£6.25

RECOLLECTIONS

Recollections

MAINLY OF WRITERS & ARTISTS

Geoffrey Grigson

CHATTO & WINDUS

THE HOGARTH PRESS

LONDON

First published in 1984 by
Chatto & Windus . The Hogarth Press
40 William IV Street
London WC2N 4DF

British Library Cataloguing in Publication Data
Grigson, Geoffrey
Recollections.
1. Authors, English – 20th century
I. Title
820.9'00912 PR106

ISBN 0 7011 2791 0

Typeset at The Spartan Press Limited
Lymington, Hants
Printed in Great Britain by
Redwood Burn Ltd
Trowbridge, Wilts

For my Family

ACKNOWLEDGEMENTS

I am grateful to Oxford University Press for allowing me to quote from the *Collected Poems* of Bernard Spencer, to Messrs Faber & Faber for quotations from the *Collected Poems* of W. H. Auden and Louis MacNeice, Messrs Hutchinson for quotations from the *Collected Poems* of Gavin Ewart, and to his representatives for poems by the late Geoffrey Taylor.

CONTENTS

My goodness, they're already starting to remember!
I thought they weren't three decades old, but now
They're fifty. Some are bald. Some launch bad breath
Across club luncheon tables, fixing labels.
Some teach. Some write lead reviews each week,
Some nest inside the littlest little magazines,
As ever. And only yesterday the whole platoon
Appeared (but not to me) so clever.
Now knowing publishers are paying them to say
How – once – they saw unlikely Orwell sporting in the hay,
Or some sly poetaster's wife caught in death's family way.

I — PROTO-PROLOGUE

The writer of these recollections, to set the frame, if not the image, straight on the wall, was born in 1905, one of the seven sons of a priest of the Church of England and a mother who was a Suffolk clergyman's daughter. He grew up in an agreeable Cornish vicarage. Climb one of the higher trees in the garden and the sea was visible between hills, blue as a hedge-sparrow's egg.

His father was sixty when he was born, a last fling for a daughter. He had emigrated from work in the Midlands and from his ancestral East Anglia, in which Grigsons had nested for several centuries in a small circle of parishes near Norwich, clerics, lawyers, doctors, content to go little further from their homes and glebes and modest estates than Bury St Edmunds, Cambridge and Norwich, which represented schooling, university and ordination. Their tablets and gravestones cluster in Norfolk churches and churchyards; and a few of the houses they built or lived in remain – in other hands. This writer's heritage, from a Grigson who matriculated at Caius College, Cambridge, in the 1570s and became Rector of Hardingham, which continued to be the centre of the family territory, was thus a very English affair.

In the later nineteenth century and in the early part of this century the family, cousins and all, broke up and scattered. Children were sent to other universities than Cambridge, and followed other callings or professions than those of their parents and ancestors. Some went to Australia, some to Ceylon and prospered more than those who stayed at home, yet all of these Grigsons retained a feeling for Norfolk, and an intermittent desire to make pilgrimages, if only to churches and gravestones.

Few of this writer's own brothers survived long in this murderous century. Three were young victims of the First World War. Two were victims of the second war, another was killed in a plane as

Commissioner for Refugees in Pakistan. They are variously buried –
a comment on their confined local ancestry – in France, Kent, India,
Burma and Rhodesia.

The writer, the seventh and last brother, educated – if that is the
term – at St John's School, Leatherhead, among the sons of the
clergy, and at Oxford instead of Cambridge, has been employed
variously as a schoolmaster, a journalist, and a publisher, and a
producer in the BBC, and then happily self-employed as a man of
letters (an old-fashioned *métier* and term?); himself three times
married, the father of four children, and the writer of many poems
and many books, who has lived for most of his life in rural Wiltshire.

His father and grandfather, who indulged in pedigrees and whose
opening tree in a family book began splendidly with Jaroslav, Duke
of Russia, and came shooting down in a folio straight line, like the lift
in the Empire State Building, to the Rev. William Grigson – but
that was a romantic Victorian affair – would be mightily surprised
to know that their descendants have married from Norway, America,
Austria, Italy, Scotland, and more or less from Holland, another
index to change.

And now the writer may revert from the Third Person Singular of
this Proto-prologue to the I of the sections which follow, mentioning
first that the reader must not expect these recollections to be set out
in a strict temporal order. As family motto one of his ancestors
adopted the phrase '*Vincit qui se Vincit*,' perhaps because he was none
too good at the art of self-conquest and was aware of it. The phrase
fits this writer as well. Far from an ordered narrative of a life through
which objectives have been held steadily in view, these recollections,
mainly of writers and artists, are glimpses, and somewhat haphazard.

2 – PROLOGUE

I

We landed from the Belfast boat at Heysham, newly married, without the rough edges and contiguous surfaces of a new relationship smoothed off, and we bought a *Daily Telegraph*, settling in the train to read through the list of flats to let; which was something worthwhile in those days. There must have been twenty or so flats listed, all within fair distance of Fleet Street, in which actual street I had found a job, and all at rents of less than £2 a week.

So began that settlement into – no, not life, but into London life, London existence, that weaning or semi-final weaning from a past which had taken us for a more or less genuine honeymoon, a climax in the old era of risky contraception, to a village in Donegal, where hay fields and potato fields sloped to a long cliff edge above the Atlantic, and where corncrakes craked monotonously and persistently into the summer night. Not far away Slieve League, William Allingham's mountain, which we climbed to the One Man's Pass, rose over the sea. Below the village, which then seemed remote to a now inconceivable degree, curved a strand up which the tide spread in the crispy pancakes of Allingham's poem, empty, when we went down to bathe, save for the oystercatchers, which rose and settled again further down the curve.

For me these weeks spent beyond the Irish railhead were in most ways familiarity newly accented, among flowers, birds and distances. For the young girl I had married, all was novel in its entirety. She was a city girl, who had grown up in St Louis, Missouri, a postgraduate student from Smith, child – urban child – of an unsuccessful attorney; whereas I was the last of the seven decidedly rural children of a clergyman in Cornwall, working at the time in the London office of a provincial daily, yet still attuned to village life, and flower-hunting and bird-watching, and small trout streams in mint-scented coombs.

3

Marriage was a weaning, as I say, a settlement. All one owned before marriage fitted into a trunk and a suitcase and a Bergen rucksack, a taxi load, with which one could flit from bed-sitter to bed-sitter, off the King's Road, or the Fulham Road, or the squalid Bloomsbury shabbiness of Theobald's Road.

The flat we picked out of the *Telegraph* was near Theobald's Road, high up, top floor, in the decay of Red Lion Square, next to a house on which a placard records that the poet and painter Rossetti once lived there. The rent was £120 a year, which seemed enormous and a rash commitment. It was one of the only flats in the square which wasn't occupied by a whore. Castor oil plants grew feebly and smuttily in the central garden. In Red Lion Passage, at one corner, a constant stink of corruption and dry rot, I would say, rose from basements. In the flat below the one we had chosen lived a coarse middle-aged loud-voiced, fattening cockney, our landlord, who ran a small fleet of green vans and lorries, with a coarse middle-aged fat wife. They were Dickensian in the blatant brutal way. I doubt if their like exists any more.

There one night Frances and I were woken by loud knocking. Outside in the wide stairs stood our landlord in a dirty night-shirt and a night-cap, shouting that he and his wife were being flooded. They were. We had left the bath tap running or dripping (the bath was in the kitchen of our three-roomed tenement). He made us descend. The overflow was coming down from the sharp tip of a light bulb, on to a double feather-bed, to one side of which our landlady, loud-mouthed as she was on occasion, also in a night-cap, was sitting up – drip, drop, drip drop – in speechless indignation. I have never forgotten that plate out of a Dickens novel or the shadows of a Dickens story televised in a Sunday serial.

2

Intellectually, or culturally, if that is the word, I felt in the early London days very immature and insecure, and in this settlement of marriage felt a need of exhibition, or justification. Had I ever met, did I think I would ever meet, any writer, painter, thinker of eminence or power? I knew about young Auden, young MacNeice, young Clere Parsons (Clere's early death deprived England of a poet who would have matured probably into genius and greatness), all three contemporaries of mine at Oxford. I knew about Eliot and the way he was still blackguarded by established intellectualism, or newspaper book-page intellectualism. But *knowing about* is distant, and knowing those of one's own age who may or may not become eminent and famous strictly by their virtues, is a privilege certainly, but one which we are apt to misjudge or misinterpret afterwards when they reach the stage of a still deserved OM or CH, or the Nobel Prize.

More self-confidence, at least, is needed during one's twenties than I possessed, to conceive that one *might* one day be in the know, person to person, junior to senior. The Cornish-East Anglian parson's son was experiencing as much as he could expect, when – or if – he glimpsed Arnold Bennett striding along Piccadilly with a whiff of April wind in his hair or Bernard Shaw waving a rolled umbrella on light step towards the London Library. Maybe I wrote poems, but I did not get them published. Maybe I reviewed a book or two for my paper (the *Yorkshire Post*), but the literary editor, such as he was, kept me short, and why should anyone else employ me?

Yet I had two strokes in particular of London luck. Before I married into settlement, I came to know, in a King's Road rooming house, a girl across the landing, a Viennese Irish Jewish girl, who in turn (she worked for an advertising agency) was befriended by an older woman in her firm who afterwards became celebrated, though she was hardly known or was in fact unknown at the time – Antonia White, exquisitely pretty, and pink, and plump (and mentally insecure). She was not, I am afraid, a very good writer, and I have always been rather surprised at the gradual accumulation of fame which established her autobiographical *Frost in May*. She was Chelsea – and a darling. She was centre to a Chelsea circle of moderately able, moderately distinguished but at least independent writers and painters – London Group painters, several of them.

I aspired by temper and rebelliousness to a different grouping, a sub-grouping, I would call, I suppose, Eliotesque, a young or junior adventurous grouping much in advance of myself whose star of magnitude was already Wystan Auden, with Stephen Spender (who would have thought, then, or later, or ever, that he would become Sir Stephen Spender?) as a star of lesser magnitude in that junior constellation.

Still I learned much (if in a timid way) from Sundays *chez* Antonia White, in which I experienced a sub-Parisian *chic*, I suppose I might call it, a Chelsea *chic*. One of this Sunday grouping, an American, Emily Holmes Coleman, introduced me (how could I have been so ignorant on my own ground?) to the journals of Dorothy Wordsworth, a life value of pure sensation, a lyrical corrective to all weakness or backsliding or dishonesty. She tore the Somerset and the Grasmere journals out of a book (Knight's edition, I suppose it must have been) and handed them to me.

My second stroke of London fortune was the presence on the London staff of the *Yorkshire Post* of a contemporary I had slightly known at Oxford, but was still rather afraid of – an intense eager-seeming character, sharp-featured and with eyes that seemed to me, rightly but also wrongly, the eyes of the Devil or one of his assistants. At the university this Gilbert Armitage had known of everyone and everything that could be characterized as modern. What happened to him in the end I have never discovered. But he was a very undevilish devil. In London his grouping was far from Chelsea. Off duty, off work, I mean, he was to be found at The Fitzroy Tavern, an acolyte of Sickert's, drinking with him and with the painter Nina Hamnett, and with the then notorious Betty May, the 'Tiger Woman', the vital creature whose autobiography he ghosted. In The Fitzroy one evening he said he had found a room in the house nearby in Howland Street where Verlaine and Rimbaud lived for a while. 'Really, Gilbert,' said Nina, 'if there's a tablet on the house to Verlaine there ought to be a tablet to me, it is the house where I lost my virginity.'

'There will be, there will be,' Sickert commented over his brandy. 'There will be a tablet at the back to Verlaine and Rimbaud, and a tablet at the front to you, my dear.'

Later on Gilbert, who from his Oxford years, as I say, knew everyone of his age who was worth knowing, produced poems grubbily written in pencil on torn bits of paper – poems by John Betjeman who was entering legend already, though the legend was a limited one still. I was in the full flush by then of admiring what literary hacks were already calling the Poets of the Thirties – Auden to be more precise – and others whom I was about to publish in my small magazine *New Verse*. One of the Betjeman poems Gilbert brought me, I remember, was 'The Arrest of Oscar Wilde at the Cadogan Hotel'. It seemed to me smart and frivolous – was that foolish or wise? – and I wouldn't publish it; which later on (or so I have been told) caused J. B. to climb from his house at Uffington and gravely curse me, standing on the backside of the White Horse above the Vale.

The important thing Gilbert did for me was to talk incessantly about a very different writer – Wyndham Lewis, and his ideas; and though the exact circumstances and details of the occasion now escape me after more than fifty years, he took me to see Lewis.

What happened to me in these early years, and then in years on the *Yorkshire Post*, followed by a time of opening sensibility – London sensibility, and that first marriage, which was to be ended by a death antibiotics would have prevented, had the illness come only a year or two later, I have described in some, if not sufficient, detail in my early autobiography *The Crest on the Silver*, which I am glad to say, has lately been reprinted, teaching me about a self and circumstances I had largely forgotten. One reviewer, I re-discover, wrote that the author was, or rather assumed the mask or character of being, an 'uneasy, bad-tempered, self-pitying emphatic egotist' – what is writing your life but egotism? – and the *Spectator* called this *Crest on the Silver* 'a shapeless book, deliberately jazzy and unsettled alike in sequence, style and substance'. I cannot say I agree, though of course I realize that the sensible or the prudent thing to do is to get on with your work and suffer the low-raters in silence. They get you even then. If you are silent about them, they call you 'exclusive'. I am afraid that some I have attacked as writers and some I have never mentioned and have therefore 'excluded', will sneer if I confess to having written *The Crest on the Silver* much under the influence of Stendhal's *Henri Brulard*; which the *Oxford Companion to French Literature* calls 'romanticized autobiography'.

Was there really a contrast or a contradiction between the Cornish childhood and getting to know of all people, all writers, this Wyndham Lewis? I think not. Here was this Cornish child, halting on his way to a favourite trout stream and sitting in the bright sunshine on a pile of road metal, which he searched for stones sparkling with black crystal, his bike leaning against the stiff cow-parsley stems beside a lane green with grass down the middle; and here he was translated to London and meeting with the author he was most to admire and finding in him the black crystal of his words. The experiences were not incompatible.

Perhaps I should add that in those days of a first entry into Lewis's secret doorway a hint, a suspicion of an interest in birds, butterflies, flowers, rarities in a vasculum, or fishing, marked one with sneering immediacy as a 'Georgian' – if one wrote, that is, or wrote poems; and there was no more despised term than 'Georgian' except among 'Georgians' themselves, whose *bête noire* was that mad intellectual fish T. S. Eliot. 'Nature', in which I lived with infinite pleasure before leaving Cornwall and childhood, was out, all round, except among Georgians.

That it should be out among the parasites – they too existed – of the New Rebellion as well as among the genuine Rebels, or so it appeared, was so much the worse for me at the time.

3 – MEETING T. S. ELIOT

And should I then presume?
And how should I begin?

Young writers are helped in the use and improvement of their gift of words if they can attach themselves to some centripetal force, some central talent, some writer who seems to them to be their time's representative of art. Such a one was Eliot, as well as Lewis; and young writers are extra lucky if as well they discover and celebrate some older influence.

To come to the rising stars of a new generation, Auden was in debt certainly to Eliot, to Eliot's encouragement, but still more he was a devotee – and imitator – of Thomas Hardy. Louis MacNeice, temperamentally attracted by the rococo, had to slough off the attractiveness of Edith Sitwell (as well as the earlier, less typographically eccentric poems of e. e. cummings); and in general it was Lewis who helped writers of my generation to realize that the Sitwells, and Edith Sitwell in particular, were not exactly art-in-earnest. The Sitwells seemed play-artists. They were smart, they were self-advertisers. Contempt for them was easy with Lewis as tutor – the Lewis of *Tarr*, and *Blast* and *Time and Western Man* and *The Art of Being Ruled*, telling us, for instance, how the Sitwells had entertained him in Venice, sweeping him in gondolas from palace to palace, church to church, gallery to gallery, never allowing him time enough to begin to take in masterpieces by Tintoretto or Bellini.

Eliot was remote, in a different way: it took nerve to edge oneself into the attention of someone so austere, poised so far away in poetic space, and so evidently learned. Perhaps by the middle Thirties profoundest respect for Eliot was beginning to be tempered a little among the young, kind as he was to them. Wasn't it Stephen Spender who remarked somewhere about this time that 'Eliot is the best we have, but what a pity he is the best'?

9

I couldn't altogether have missed that Grand Cham of Poetry – of the New Poetry. Yet I came first of all to meet, if not to know Eliot, because of family and not literary circumstances. My young wife's family belonged to Eliot's St Louis, Missouri. 'So you are Tom Galt's daughter.' Those were the first words I heard Eliot speak. Had I quite realized it, that was a slightly pregnant remark, since my father-in-law back in St Louis was rather a rogue, an appalling failure of an attorney who ruined an inherited law practice, and managed, after his wife's death because of frail health or by drowning (on purpose and in despair?) to embezzle or squander most of her money. The Galts and the Eliots lived in the same Van der Venter Place in St Louis, and Tom Galt and Tom Eliot went for a while to the same school.

'So you are Tom Galt's daughter' – the occasion of that remark was a formal summertime tea in the upstairs flat in South London of an elderly friend of Eliot's, a novelist with false black hair and a large bosom and a glittering ebony eye. Gossip said she had once lived with H. G. Wells. Her son-in-law, when I knew her, was Litvinov, the Soviet foreign minister, who had married her daughter Ivy; and this Alice Herbert's predatory eye was open always for young men about London who might develop (she hoped) as writers whose vitalizing or revitalizing acquaintance she could claim.

I am afraid, though, that she was a slightly ridiculous over-eager person, high-collared (whalebone-collared) like my own mother, out of an Edwardian past.

Through Alice Herbert's drawing-room window on the first floor (she had been Alice Low, and so the mother of Ivy Low) we had looked down through the plane trees and watched the arrival of the Eliots. He emerged from an Austin Seven, or rather there first emerged a little Pomeranian lap-dog and then the eccentric Mrs Eliot, who proved to be uncommonly like a difficult irritable Pomeranian herself, given to yapping and sudden pointless incursions into the tea-time conversation about St Louis and other matters which polite thin Eliot was carrying on with this pink and pretty daughter of a foolish Tom Galt.

'Why?' she would suddenly say, 'Why?', and balancing his tea-cup or his thin bread-and-butter or cucumber sandwich Eliot would patiently explain why. That this Englishwoman was Eliot's cross was true unquestionably.

Such a grouping as I belonged to, or attached myself to, began in earnest just a little later than this not very encouraging first encounter, when I founded the 'little magazine', *New Verse*.

4 – WYNDHAM LEWIS

The man I am to exact what is due to men,
The man I am to exact it only with the pen.

*

These times require a tongue that naked goes,
Without more fuss than Dryden's, or Defoe's.

Lewis was already famous, book after book coming from him, when I reached London, far too big a man, too intellectually insistent and self-sure, however physically shy, to allow himself to be hidden by an ineffectual modesty. He was the combative intellectual under the wide black hat crushed over his darkened forehead and black-framed spectacles, known for witty, actively devastating verbs in controversy and destructive adjectives contributing to brilliant images and metaphors; also for being inaccessible except through the Piccadilly Safe Deposit. He was a Central Londoner who didn't believe it 'safe' to live farther away than Notting Hill Gate, the Enemy in public, or at least in print, and the secret man in private – Herbert Read to Lewis encountered by the ticket machines of the Piccadilly Underground, just after the publication of Lewis's *One Way Song*: 'I didn't know you wrote verse, Lewis' (but he ought to have known); Lewis sardonically to Read (whose few rather flaccid long poems – and short ones – he despised, and whom he despised as one who theorized about painting and never looked a picture, he said, in the face): 'I never knew it was so damned easy, Read.'

I can imagine, from many other occasions, the amused glint in his eyes which would have gone with that reply. Words amused him, condemnation, an intellectual matter, never a sour or vindictive one, amused him as he uttered it. That amused look with some devastating comment or summary, was one of the most delightful, seductive things about his company.

My first meeting with Lewis *à deux*, without Gilbert Armitage, a meeting to which I had been summoned by telegram, was in an ABC tea-room near Leicester Square, and not far from Zwemmer's book-shop, to which he often went, he and Anton Zwemmer having much in common, about painting at least, and in their strong self-certainties. Lewis had exquisite manners, even face to face with people – people of the writing world whom he disliked for the best of reasons – but he was not given to small talk, sardonic and humorous talk maybe, but never clucking about nothing. My recollection of tea and buns with him in that ABC is that he at once launched into questions.

What did I know about Goya? Had I read Gogol, had I read Conrad, and Henry James? Had I much sympathy for Virginia Woolf's kind of writing or the kind of writing by his friend Joyce, from whom alas, Virginia Woolf's soft flow derived? Did I care much for most Bloomsbury writers, and painters, for the Bloomsbury assumption of being English literature of the day, or for such Bloomsbury acolytes and trumpeters as Cyril Connolly? Did I know Bradley's *Truth and Reality*?

A man at the next table suddenly collapsed and fell dead. His body was moved aside and whisked out of the crowded ABC with astonishing speed. Lewis made a remark or two about the twentieth-century way in which we don't leave death lying about, but cover it up bodily, at once, as if it never happened; and back he went to the questions and admonitions. This immediacy of approach was very much Lewis's way. A year or two later, for instance, at the time of the huge exhibition of British Art at Burlington House, I sat down with Lewis and Henry Moore in the comfy basement of the Cadena (upstairs he wouldn't sit: it was too public). Lewis was curious – more than curious – about Henry Moore. We had talked about, or rather he had talked to me about Moore and he knew we were friends. No preliminaries, no small talk. A moment's nervousness as the tea arrived, and Lewis launched into questions about how Moore carved, how he attacked wood or stone, elm wood, and lime? And the kinds of stone? Did Moore make plaster sketches (which he certainly did not in those days, in accord with a new art puritanism or severity which despised the inherited white conventions of Burlington House and commemorative portraiture and statuary).

Lewis was satisfied, and Moore too. In those years the gentler Moore was another maligned rebel or maligned individualist, and sympathised more immediately with this stronger rebel, who had so few words to waste. The Enemy he might be, but how far he was from mere negation and combativeness. And for Lewis two or three cups of tea and a round or two of hot buttered toast were enough to confirm Moore's knowledge and active profundity.

A successful tea. The black hat was resumed and Lewis disappeared, anonymous, into the dark crowdedness of Piccadilly. I am not sure that they ever met again.

Looking back, I see that Lewis was certainly prepared to cultivate or even flatter people, older or younger, who might be useful to his books, and here was I now editing the book pages of a national daily. But I don't know that such cultivation was other than a venial process, and Lewis – how wonderful it was to know him, how flattering too – was a poor man, never for sale, who had to live – somehow – by his books, his occasional writings and his painting, none of which were ever popular.

I came to know Lewis in his late middle age, tall, handsome, delicate fingered, if in a way timid except in his wonderful gift of written and spoken images. His stories – like most sensible people, he was amused by gossip about people who interested or concerned him if the gossip fitted – were ribald; his language, exquisite manners or no, courteous host or no, could be raw, spontaneously or with calculation. How surprising it often was, the vigorous strong verb, the vigorous strong adjective. It was unkind, certainly when kindness was hardly called for, though seldom other than his own and memorable and funny – in private especially, since Lewis knew and cared more than most for the proprieties of art, without the attendant falsities by which so much is evaded or softened. Early in his writing and painting days he had nothing to live on for a while but a weekly sum of money contributed by better-off friends who admired him. He needed it, and hated to take it. He hated the way it came to him, in cash, generally by the hand of Fanny Wadsworth, whom he didn't much care for (with some reason – a physical reason so far as I remember). She was rich, or at least her husband Edward Wadsworth, the artist, was rich, reputed inheritor of a fortune of £900,000. Anyway, there came a week when no dumpy or rather tarted-up and ill-tempered looking Fanny Wadsworth arrived, and no money arrived, Lewis at the time being in particular need. Wadsworth and Fanny next day received a postcard, on which Lewis had scrawled, in his rather scratchy black script, only five words,

Where's the fucking stipend?
Lewis.

I know pious friends, ex-friends, or somewhat ex-admirers of Lewis who profess themselves shocked by that once famous p.c., proclaiming that it reveals just what was wrong with Lewis's character and conduct.

No doubt they would have felt the same about another verbal occasion. He was living in a very comfortable secret flat not a great way from Paddington, to which a few at any rate of his younger friends were sometimes admitted for a winter tea. But Lewis liked to be master or bidder of his own entertainment, and one afternoon I and another of his younger friends, Hugh Gordon Porteous, we two alone, were bidden. I arrived to find a third guest unbidden, having much to say and eating his lavishly buttered scones on his black and white striped sofa. She was the friend of Hugh Porteous. Lewis had never met her and never wanted to meet her – admittedly she was an ugly, rather bug-like little body, her dress and look conveyed rather a hint of lesbianism. Lewis, as at other times, was talking of Spain, and Goya and the Prado, and of the miraculously huge scale of the great Goyas and paintings up to the ceilings by Velasquez which we see so often only in the small misleading confines of a book.

The little bug-like person chattered on about Spain, in a way all too knowing and too trivial. Lewis treated her with his usual fine courtesy, slightly exaggerated, I half thought at the time. Porteous and his girl left, Lewis exploded briefly. 'How did *she* get to Spain' (Spain was too far off and too expensively far off for most of us at the time) 'unless she sucked her way there?' The verb was his own, as the phrase was, more politely, but not with less startling effect, when he called the character in his novel *Tarr*, whom he based on the Bloomsburyite Clive Bell, a 'scarecrow of an advanced fool-farm' (he was portrayed wearing an art-uniform) or referred to fat G. K. Chesterton, body and some attitudes in one, as a 'fierce foaming toby-jug'.

How well I remember other summonses and occasions – another invitation to a meal in another cosy flat, after he returned to London from his wartime sojourn in Canada (strictly he was a Canadian citizen). 'There is' were his words, surprisingly, 'a big white bull-terrier' – was the bull-terrier Lewis's friend or the special friend of his gentle, rather silent, rather long-suffering, patient wife? – 'and there are large honey-coloured lakes supplying us with what they have always lacked. His mistress is Nero's wife. Please come, suitably shod, to tea or to dinner.'

Or I recall an earlier occasion, when Stephen Spender and I were ordered to a secret London studio (I think he was being pursued at the time for debt) with nothing pinned up in the dark along a corridor but 'Lewis' and a number. Inside, furniture there was none except three armchairs in front of a comfortable fire, a bottle of whisky and some glasses on a packing-case (he did his writing at that time and kept his library at another secret address for fear of seizure), in the gathering gloom behind us, half lit by a single bulb, another packing-case, and some paints and brushes and an easel. Then the Lewis monologue – almost his monologue – began with courteous intervals for either of us to interject a word or an opinion.

Another occasion. In one of the theatrical alcoves of that now vanished coloured palace of Frascati's in High Holborn (Lewis in funds for once), an announcement, with a reading, of the existence of *One Way Song*, which was shortly to be published. The reading was punctuated with a sardonic remark or two on changes which T. S. Eliot (his special friend and publisher at Faber & Faber) wanted him to make for what Eliot conceived to be the sake of propriety. From time to time Lewis re-filled and held up a vivid glass of crême-de-menthe, till it caught the light and glowed, Lewis, though he owned to a sweet tooth, liking the green as much as the taste.

As to my own attitude or relation to this great man, one of course chooses one's heroes – and a hero of mine he certainly was for a long while – to some degree by temperament. For some of my friends in the Thirties the proper hero was T. S. Eliot, whose blood certainly ran a little thin, for others the proper illuminant was the tenderness and toughness and clear-sightedness of E. M. Forster. Yet in Lewis simply as a writer, simply in the words cut in a high crisp relief across the page, there showed a militancy and courage extra-attractive to any young rebelliousness of the literary mind. If art was more than a game cooked up by fashion or by the spirit of the age, if art mattered, then here, long before I understood all or half of what Lewis meant by art, shone clearer than a comet hanging in the midnight sky Art's Champion.

Lewis was the first great man I ever encountered. How exciting to know about him, how extra exciting to know him as well. What fun to hear some of the fruitier gossip about artists and writers two to three generations older than the young of one's own time, to hear about Lewis consulting Sickert about what to do for clap. 'Nothing,' Sickert said. He had had several doses – it was 'no worse than a cold in the nose', advice Lewis took with carelessness and ill consequences – imagine Eliot having clap. How intriguing of Augustus John in his student days rumbustiously attempting to board respectable girls in families Lewis was on the best of polite terms with – for instance in a Dorset vicarage – like a clumsy buccaneer, or to be told Lewis's story of coming one day through the open door of Eliot's flat and finding Lady Ottoline Morrell, in pearl necklaces, on her knees, that long lamp-post of a woman, saying 'Teach me how to pray, Tom.' How healthy to be helped to feel for a time above the daily accidents and chores and even the affections of young existence, to find that Lewis too had picked out for his admiration the poems of younger Auden and MacNeice – to sense that one was on a right track.

'You have more children, I hear,' said Lewis when we met after a longish interval. 'Unwise. I have no children' – was that true? –

'though some, I believe are attributed to me. I have work to do.' So he had – work of every kind from writing, to thinking, talking, painting: the work of existing too.

I confess to having had, not a period of anti-Lewis, but a period almost of despondency when it seemed for a while that so much of the higher modernism was fragmented and left incomplete, and especially when the intellectual milieu of the Hampstead Thirties, which looked up to such as Eliot and Lewis, was in a way shattered by the war. I wrote a sonnet with this in mind, yet leaving such readers as it might have, to guess (according to person) those, or their work, that I had in mind:

> *They were the saints and heroes of my early age;*
> *And one, deep in that cusped and coloured*
> *Restaurant, read me his words about the page*
> *Torn from the shut book: he was untainted*
>
> *For me even by his errors, and full perfection*
> *Seemed in wide possession of his sky,*
> *Silvered them like virtues, past detection*
> *By my rebellious and imperfect eye.*
>
> *I do not now reject them: incomplete,*
> *In this quiet full-moon'd September night*
> *Their wisdom warns me of the soft and white,*
> *A moron scratching, and the aimless feet:*
>
> *I want perfection; but this cooler light*
> *No longer shows it in a debris of defeat.*

But now, looking back, how much less sure I would be about the role or possibility of perfection, about the debris of defeat.

In his way Lewis, this man of fullness and fun, of a Rabelaisian appetite (Rabelais had a sinewy critical intelligence after all), with his delight in words and situations and the bizarre, hated with effect all that interfered with the proper energies and employment of embodied mind, and I should round off, thinking about him once more after so many years, with a reminder of what the concept of art implied for him.

He thought none too cheerfully that our age was in danger of becoming the first age in our history, our human history, of 'men without art'. Art was more than its manifestation in this painting or that poem. 'The artist,' Lewis says in one of his books, 'is relieved of that obligation of the practical man to lie', art was the act of that man the artist delivered from the practical man's need of jogging along by telling lies. It was the prime enemy both of mere life or living, and of death: it was hard, sharp, conceptual, the thing made by flesh-bound man at his best, his most pure, and most conscious moments.

Genius he called 'the greatest development of conscious person-ality'. He might agree that art is 'a spell, a talisman, an incantation'; but if for him art was 'the civilized substitute for magic', just 'as philosophy is what, on a higher or more complex plane, takes the place of religion', Lewis was for ever setting against the equivocal, against the public opinion mind, against the surging, the too ecstatic and the featureless, that which has features, that which has exactitude and harmonious proportion, that which was the construc-tion of consciousness and not 'the gushing of undisciplined life.' He said art consisted of 'the noblest intellectual exercises of the Animal, Man'; take away those intellectual exercises, take away art, and what would be left except an animal – a rat – merely a little more clever than other animals?

It is a question of perennial gravity, but it was and it remains very much a question of our time, when position after position is surrendered to a mindless pressure of numbers.

I cannot think that for all the revival of interest in him Lewis will ever be a popular author. He was too profound a humanist.

He had no kindly twinkle in his eye, and no wish that anyone should ever ascribe that twinkle to him. If he indeed twinkled, which isn't really the word, if a slow and to be sure a most attractive smile played across his eyes and his mouth, you needed to realize what he was up to, and take no liberties. The slow smile across his eyes and mouth was attractive, to be sure: he was being amused satirically perhaps by something in the situation, some quick thought, some all-of-a-sudden recollection or realization. What he wasn't doing was including *you* in affection, like a kindly public figure putting on his professional smile, or like a kindly uncle humouring a nephew. He wasn't being soppy and charitable, or unbending like someone exercising his familiar charm on the television screen: at the most he would be intimating that you would of course be as damned silly as the rest of us. When he was young, he wrote a piece he called *The Code of the Herdsman*, in which he spoke of the mountain where the artist must be his own caste, raised above the valley of the terrible processions into which he must descend, but out of which he must climb again. 'Our sacred hill', he wrote in that very short credo, 'is a volcanic heaven. But the result of its violence is peace.'

It will be all violence, if the words of such rare men as Lewis are overlooked: it will not be peace at all.

A story is told of Lewis's last descent, old, sick, blind, into hospital, not long before his death. Aware into the bargain that her new patient was of some eminence or importance, the sympathetic matron lent over his bed and asked her customary question: 'And when did we last open our bowels, Mr Lewis?'

Lewis, the individualist, in charge of himself to the end, is said to have replied 'Mind your own bloody business', and turned over. Apocryphal? I wouldn't think so, entirely. All I would doubt among his last recorded words, is that word 'bloody' – that breach of manners to the innocent, unless Lewis felt trapped at last.

5 – CLERE PARSONS

We are not yet collected works, my dear.

I have no doubt that a nearly entire oblivion or neglect has obscured many poets in our times as in times past, good poets if not great ones, ones who were not inclined to blow their own trumpets, or ones who died young. Finding them, recognizing them, attempting to break the hard shell of neglect or indifference or ignorance around them is one of the pleasures of habitual incursions into the huge territory of English writing. In her own country New Zealanders, for instance, don't seem to make much of the garden poet Evelyn Hayes. At home, though she goes on writing with increasing skill and perhaps unfashionable tenderness, we don't make much of an Oxford contemporary, Joy Scovell, and I have in mind one other poet who died young (and whose name I have mentioned) and whose poems, a single pamphlet of them collected after his death by Herbert Read, has special concern for myself at any rate and only a few others of my own age.

Could you, could many proud of knowing about the poetry of the last five or six decades say without hesitation who wrote the following:

> *Living from day to day provides no clue*
> *For certain happiness – it is a shallow*
> *Youngster philosophy and easy to see through*
> *Sirs, we know what usually it comes to –*
> *The drunkard's bliss, the braggadoccio*
>
> *'Admire me now triumphant over virtue'*
> *The rake's bravado and tedious libido*
> *Gin in small hours, praise for the cunning ruse*
>
> *Nor can you live by glimpses of the 'True'*
> *And 'Beautiful', snapshotting scenery;*
> *However slick, neither will the kodak do*

See gaunt and curt to luminary sky
Rear the gas drums the guardians of the city
– But emblems of elder power have passed by

Survey the ruined bridge, the crumbled tower,
Now homes for owls the desiccated trees
Which threw deep shade for feudal ladies leafless
Conjure the past from books of history

Reveal the narrow lusts the mean the sour
Rancid intrigues, the base servility

And till the day of doom continue too
Heads in the sand ostriches in a row
Far easier so, to do as others do.

The poem was called 'Living from Day to Day Provides no Clue', a title which assuredly does provide a clue, and the writer was another Oxford contemporary of mine, a long, pale-faced boy, a Christ Church undergraduate and graduate, Clere Parsons, who died when he was twenty-three, in 1931.

Ironically he had written, in another poem, 'We are not yet collected works, my dear'. But he very soon was, between covers of brilliant lemon, eighteen poems collected, as I say, by Herbert Read, and published by Eliot.

'Poems by Clere Parsons, Born 1908, died 1931' – that is all it prints on the title page without a word elsewhere, – without a word of introduction. A mistake to have added so little, since posterity does like something of a biographical legend – more than a name, and all biographies are legend more or less – to attach to the work of a poet, all the more if he dies young.

Saying too little invited an oblivion.

I myself have one special, even pictorial, memory of Clere Parsons, which I shall come to in a minute, repeating meanwhile that Clere Parsons might have been no less of a master than those other Oxford contemporaries of his, and mine, Louis MacNeice and Wystan Auden.

His friend John Davenport, who was at school with him at St Paul's, told me the tale of his unnecessary death. He was a diabetic, dependent on his injections of insulin, and as if he felt he might not have a great many years to live, he was sure that he must live those years with enjoyment, sensual, emotional and intellectual (he took a first in history). In lodgings in winter, in Oxford, having come down there from London about a job he was offered in the Bodleian Library, he caught a chill, the chill turned to pneumonia, he was wrapped up and taken off to hospital, and died there in a coma from lack of insulin, no one having a clue to his diabetes. He was one of three brothers, and his father was an Indian Civil Servant who had also died young. One brother was a naval officer, one was in the army.

Oddly he was only slightly acquainted with Wystan Auden, of his own college, and he did not know Louis MacNeice, across the back lane in Merton College, though you could say that he belonged, or would have seemed to belong, to the MacNeice school of poetry.

He dreamed, lived and travelled poetry in that short space between graduation and death. Beginning with an admiration for Flecker and in homage always to Donne, he quickly discovered not only rococo poets of his day including e. e. cummings, but the French masters, travelling to the Mediterranean and reading, Davenport remembered, *Le Cimetière Marin* on the spot, in Valéry's gleaming sun-brilliant cemetery sloping to the sea, going to Charleville to do homage to Rimbaud, discovering Baudelaire and Mallarmé in Paris, and Proust at Chartres, and Illiers –

> *Mallarmé for a favour*
> *teach me to achieve*
> *the rigid gesture won only with labour*
> *and comparable to the ease*
> *balance and strength with which the ballet-dancer*
> *sustains her still mercurial pose in air*

– discovering painters as well:

Now joy's cartographer I trace
My acres of gay and wellbeing's land
O my summer be music be Proust and Sisley and
With me in the dead season, pastoral days.

I don't know what his beliefs were – except that he was surprisingly the most political of the Thirties poets, keeping the politics very much to himself. When, in the late Sixties, I tried to discover facts about Clere from as many of his contemporaries as I could trace, only one of them had a word to say of him as a political animal, a first poet of the Thirties to idealize the communism of Russia. All the same I am sure he was too cultured and too intelligent ever to behave as naively as Cecil Day-Lewis, ever to ask in a poem, as Day-Lewis did, 'Yes, why do we all, seeing a Red, feel small,' and I see in his poems, however he began, the development of lyrical intellect, I see in them a Spinoza-like sense of joy and the value and necessity of joy, balancing, or rather accompanying, a not unnaturally ominous quality.

I come now to my own special memory of Clere Parsons, who was some three years my junior. Now and again I had encountered him, I had spoken to him once or twice, but didn't know him. What I have had floating in my mind for more than fifty years is the sight of young Clere Parsons, tall, very thin, pallid, fair-haired, a trifle spotty, and aloof (as he always seemed), leaning forward and passing through the vestibule of an office in Bloomsbury, the office in Russell Square which contained T. S. Eliot. With him was a shorter, dark girl, Sonia Hambourg, daughter of Mark Hambourg the pianist whom he was going to marry (and who became in the end a nun in a Russian nunnery outside Paris, guarding the memory of that first love of hers whose death had shattered her for a while).

For me, still, seen more clearly than the circumstances or the occasion, is that very young face, with lips which curled with a slightly curious authority (that was the effect, though the curl of the lips was caused by a tooth projecting a little out of line). I have always connected that sight of him with the first view one gets of the Peak of Tenerife, rootless and floating in the air. I have thought of his few

24

accessible poems as flying fish that break out of the sea around Tenerife and glint, and enter the sea again starboard and larboard of a ship's bows – as if the poems were in some measure driven out of him by the approach of death.

> *Some melody of words continues on*
> *Over and above the words in which I think*
> *And which the outer being is based on*
>
> *If once within the bounds of meaning it came*
> *I might enclose within a verbal system*
> *This opulent lovely tongue that has no name*
>
> *No rules of grammar, no place for adverb*
> *No active and passive, no paradigm*
> *Not even the primal and primordial verb*
>
> *It is the original rhythm whence speech sprung*
> *The dog feels too before the fire which burns*
> *These crazy flames his deft thought leaps among.*

He left behind him few people to remember and care for his poems, or even to claim ownership of his copyrights, this word poet and rhythm poet, and poet of shape, holding the function and matter of his verse so intelligently in view.

Interpret or assess this writer in your own way, if you seek him out in the Bodleian or in the British Library (which turned him down on the grounds of health) or if you are lucky enough to find a copy of that lemon yellow pamphlet. I shall only reiterate that after so many decades I continue to think of him with regret; and continue to find an 'opulent lovely tongue' in him, his personal rhythm, in poems which are exquisite, grave, artificial, and permanent.

6 – NEW VERSE

Miss Twye was soaping her breasts in the bath
When she heard behind her a meaning laugh
And to her amazement she discovered
A wicked man in the bathroom cupboard.

Gavin Ewart, in *New Verse*

Looking back through *New Verse*, as the once young man who began it and published the first number in January 1933 and carried it on for six years, I re-discover with some relief that it was not too solemn a periodical. I dislike recalling a rude and rough, if sometimes quite funny bullying which became one of its characteristics after two or three years. But the circumstances explain, if they do not altogether excuse, such asperities. The public and official provinciality of the time in London (a condition we seem to be restoring in 1984), and in the universities, in spite of Joyce, Lewis and Eliot, and Eliot's *Criterion*, remained more than usually extreme. The educational establishment no less than the book pages of the Sunday papers and the 'serious' weeklies still conducted an elderly witch hunt against 'modernism' in art or letters. For instance I remember a don at All Souls, Canon Hutchinson, editor, for the Oxford University Press, of the best edition of the poems of the great George Herbert, intimating blandly over the college port that the Master of University College, Sir Michael Sadler, was both silly and eccentric because he owned incomprehensible pictures by Kandinsky and placed a white figure by Henry Moore (whom he had helped and encouraged in his Leeds days) in the window of his house on Boars Hill. Also I recall shouting into the ear – this would have been two or three years after the founding of *New Verse* – of a small deaf director of the Leicester Galleries that it was time he staged an exhibition of Paul Klee, whose work had never been seen in England.

'What's that? What's that?' – his hand to his ear – 'Klee, Klee?

26

wouldn't sell one of them.' Discovering about Klee, in London, meant going up the road to Zwemmer's bookshop, which was so powerful an influence in the Thirties and Forties, and scouting around for some small imported Klee album or pamphlet.

Going back to the genesis of *New Verse*, it was stuffiness of that kind which had led to a tea-time discussion one afternoon in the ground floor flat of No. 4 Keats Grove, between myself, Hugh Ross-Williamson, and my wife, that young post-graduate student from Smith College and from the St Louis, Mo., and even the Van der Venter Place, of T. S. Eliot.

We talked about the Situation. Every virtuous 'little magazine' needs to be the outcome of a Situation, which makes the young promoters of such a magazine indignant – and enthusiastic.

Here, I think, Hugh Ross-Williamson was more innocent than myself. Ego is liable to be active in the birth of little magazines. Here was I wanting recognition or something to be recognized for. Here was I writing poems, and wanting somewhere to publish them. Here was I earning a living at the time by editing the book pages of the *Morning Post*, that right-wing, ultra-right-wing daily which in the end was to be absorbed in the ultra-right-wing *Daily Telegraph*. It was ten years, in that birth-year of *The Orators* by the young Auden and of *New Verse*, since Eliot had published *The Waste Land*, and my bosses, my Tory bosses on that in some ways admirable, in some ways deplorable and disreputable daily paper had noticed no author, no poet certainly, since Kipling (the editor, H. A. Gwynne, was one of Kipling's friends) and no poem by Kipling other than 'If' or 'Gunga Din'. Wouldn't it be ironic, and pleasurable, to use the money from selling surplus review copies every week (the literary editor's perquisite) to pay for printing and distributing a poetry magazine of a stripe so different from that of the *Morning Post* (or of a stripe so different from that of every publisher of the day other than Faber's, of which Eliot was a director so generous to young poets)?

Hugh Ross-Williamson did not write poems, so far as I know. Through family connections (he too had a living to earn) he was the young, new editor of the impossibly bookish and frumpish old

Bookman, which he was struggling to reform and bring from the ruling belleslettrism into the twentieth century. Moreover Hugh had just published one of the first books – if not the very first one? on the poems of T. S. Eliot, Aunt Sally of the middle-brows. An evidence of the Situation of 1932 and 1933 may be read in the last words of Hugh's last chapter: 'It will be found, I dare to prophesy, that T. S. Eliot will be recognized generally as one of the very few great writers of the post-war world.'

Even that accolade seemed a way off and premature. And what I have called the Situation was multiplex, multipolar, or multi-siliquous. Unrecognized generally as he may have been, yet approachable for his juniors, ambiguous Mr Eliot, down in Russell Square, was, after all, already beginning to be seen by those juniors, or by some of them, as I have mentioned, as an elder of modernism, even just a little *vieux jeu*.

Wyndham Lewis under his black hat (Desmond McCarthy had long ago called him 'that sulky tinker' – which wasn't a misprint for 'thinker'), invisible in Notting Hill, or in a secret Kensington studio or scarcely visible on a risky visit to Zwemmer's bookshop in Charing Cross Road, or disembodied altogether behind a box number in the Piccadilly Safe Deposit, stood for a less ambiguous energy, for the intellectual passion Yeats admired in him, though hardly for democratic or E. M. Foster-ian love. Joyce, Yeats himself – their feet had already been seen disappearing into an Empyrean, *vis-à-vis* the young, or into something of an Elsewhere. 'Bearded Ezra', Ezra Pound, began to seem zany except to the zany, and sent his cards in a rude raspberry shorthand from Rapallo, and was, after all, and despite Eliot's talk of him as *il miglior fabbro* (and *pace* our present academics), not much of a poet.

A second newness was arriving. As I say the planet Auden was up, at least on the edge of the sky; and the year of our tripartite tea-time discussion in Keats Grove was the year of more than *The Orators*. Remarkable poems by Stephen Spender continued to appear (his *Poems* also belong to this birth-year of *New Verse* – both *The Orators* and Spender's *Poems* were to be advertised by Faber's on the last page of *New Verse* No. 1). Louis MacNeice, last seen stalking in a cloak in the dusk of the purlieus of Merton College, was away in Birmingham teaching Greek, and writing poems now much less Twentyish and Sitwellian than any that had appeared in his one book so far, his *Blind Fireworks*. Clere Parsons, so likely to have proved the most sparkling and, next to Auden, most intelligent poet among his coevals, was unhappily dead, but his *Poems* (1932) were out, and were in our thoughts in that garden room in Keats Grove where we concluded that a second newness needed a new magazine, which could sensibly (since names take their colour from what they name) be called *New Verse*.

So not long afterwards *New Verse* No. 1 appeared – two poems by MacNeice, one by Auden –

> *I have a handsome profile*
> *I've been to a great public school*
> *I've a little money invested*
> *Then why do I feel such a fool*
> *As if I owned a world that had had its day?* . . .

(no punctuation marks, you will see, except the question mark which finished the stanza: we were 'modern'), a piece by I. A. Richards on D. H. Lawrence's *Last Poems*, and another by Herbert Read on Gerard Manley Hopkins, the generations, wherever the emphasis lay, well mixed.

Price 6*d*. 'The price of . . . a brief library borrowing of *Angel Pavement*' (which was J. B. Priestley's latest novel).

Here and there that hatchet gleamed in such a premonitory phrase. But to offset the blade here in *New Verse* No. 1 was – deliberately – that I. A. Richards, our respected elder, who had taught some of us (see his little book *Science and Poetry*) about Thomas Hardy: here he was quoting Coleridge on not introducing 'an Act of Uniformity against poets', a caveat, some people may be surprised to hear, seldom out of the editor's mind in the next six years, or since. At the same time a pervading concern in *New Verse* was to hope and work for a poetry – or for poems – particular, individual, palpable, which was free of the overlapping poeticism inherited from the long century in which drowsy numbness had seemed so often to be the absolute rule.

We knew John Crowe Ransom (whose verse, at once so unAmerican and unEnglish, had been introduced to us by Robert Graves and was on sale in Harold Monro's Poetry Bookshop near the British Museum, if nowhere else in those days).

Sing a song for Percy Shelley,
Drowned in pale lemon jelly.

And for precious John Keats,
Dripping blood of pickled beets.

Years and years later I read that one of the directing powers of the BBC who had taken a first in Greats and so loathed the coming of the Third Programme and worked for its abolition, was given to reciting in self-defence the whole of Matthew Arnold's 'Dover Beach'. Or at least – *furled-world*. 'And we are here as on a darkling plain' – he did so on one anxious walk between Regent's Park and Broadcasting House. A great poem, to be sure; but one which could be misapplied. *New Verse* – editor's egoism and all – was planned to promote a cleaner and fresher poetry, and to promote more than pleasure, or sadness, in the 'wet, wet lay'. In parallel, wasn't my Hampstead friend and neighbour Henry Moore insistent on carving, on cutting wood and stone, instead of pushing clay or plasticine?

After so many years it is difficult for me to recall the detail or the mechanics of running *New Verse* (for which, let me tell American university librarians even today, no papers or accounts remain). I should say nevertheless that it owed something – something – in promotion and appearance to a degree of professionalism. Little magazines suggest as a rule – not to mention what is in them – a happy rustic ignorance of type, proof, paper, and make-up. Hugh Ross-Williamson (though his role was only one of discussion and suggestion and encouragement) and I were at any rate professional journalists who had served together on the *Yorkshire Post*.

In pursuit of good printing and unobtrusive efficiency of look by the standards of the time, I went to another ex-member of the staff of the *Yorkshire Post*, Brooke Crutchley, of the Cambridge University Press. So *New Verse* looked well, looked more grown up than it was, coverless, and immediate, with its name across in sky-blue ink above the list of contents.

When the copy for No. 3 reached Cambridge, it was found to include 'Phallus in Wonderland' (by a young Gavin Ewart, undelivered still, I think I am right in saying, from the sixth form in Wellington College). The title invited a look at the first stanza:

> *Prima coitio est acerrima (Terence);*
> *In 1889 I first encountered woman*
> *And copulated unsatisfactorily*
> *Owing to ignorance*

– which was a little too much for the Cambridge University Press. The times were different. Numbers 3 and 4 of *New Verse* had to go to another Cambridge Printer. No. 5 (the bold title words NEW VERSE having changed back to blue, after blue then changed to green, and then to red – for no political reason) went to the considerate and kindly book-printing house of Billing and Sons at Guildford, who never pressed for immediate payment, and printed *New Verse* year by year without scruples until it came to an end in May 1939.

After No. 2 we were able (but not because of rip-roaring sales) to pay contributors. By No. 8 (April 1934, the war still five years ahead) contributors had come to include (as well as Auden and MacNeice) Cecil Day Lewis, George Barker, William Empson, Theodore Spencer, Allen Tate, Charles Madge, Norman Cameron, Edwin Muir (a neighbour up the hill from Keat's Grove), Stephen Spender, A. J. M. Smith, Humphrey House, David Gascoyne, Dylan Thomas, Kathleen Raine, and Robert Hamer (who directed *Kind Hearts and Coronets*); and *New Verse* was impinging – and causing irritation – beyond the confines of a minority magazine's expected range. (John Masefield, by the way, then Poet Laureate, and Wallace Stevens in America, were among the only poet-subscribers –

31

subscribers not contributors – from an older generation). Evidently *New Verse* had been picked up by that clever, rather time-serving journalist Ivor Brown, who wrote in a book, *I Commit to the Flames*, that if something or other did not quench readers' appetite (for modernism, I think he meant) they could 'try *New Verse* which erupts at sixpence a time every two months from a nicely chosen address in Keats Grove, Hampstead ("where Keats heard the nightingale, you know")'. It had been picked up too, by John Sparrow, the future Warden Sparrow, already a Fellow of All Souls, who wrote of the influence of Ezra Pound's *Mauberly* apparent in a stanza he quoted 'from a 200-line poem, entitled (I suppose wittily) *Phallus in Wonderland* and printed in Cambridge which claims to represent all the valuable elements in contemporary poetry.' The claim was a fiction of John Sparrow's. *New Verse*, i.e. the editor, commented that the book in which he made the claim, was printed in Glasgow, and headed its counter-comment *Matthew XXIX, 10*. I always hoped that learned and charming John Sparrow consulted his New Testament.

Certainly *New Verse* was taking or had taken a combative turn I do not much like to recall. It was salutary then or then abouts to have in mind Wyndham Lewis's *One Way Song*:

> *These times require a tongue that naked goes*
> *Without more fuss than Dryden's or Defoe's.*

But Lewis was at hand to say that one should select one's quarry with a proper respect for advancing principles, and not be trivially combative.

Was it trivial to go for the Desmond McCarthy streak in English letters? Perhaps. Or to go for puritan Leavis and *Scrutiny*?

'Mr Leavis, it seems, cannot recognize creative generosity until years have passed; one likes to think how stiffly he would have reviewed Lawrence's only novels. Dr Leavis and *Scrutiny* are sincere, but sincerity by itself is not a very useful thing; and *Scrutiny*, if Dr Leavis wants some plain criticism is too adolescent, too self-righteous, too ready to accept the naiveties of ledger-criticism informed with a little sour yeast of Eliot and Lawrence. It sets up taste as a humanist idol, and so inspired prints in the present number a poem which should easily have been detected as a vulgar and empty derivation from the methods of Eliot. If *Scrutiny* is not to be the perfect body-builder for prigs, it must change its formula.'

New Verse, No. 4, 1933

Trivial perhaps? I mean too trivial a quarry altogether? But I still think of that 'perfect body-builder for prigs' without repentance, and precisely as I wrote of it when I was twenty-eight.

Meanwhile there was always the physical business of running and distributing *New Verse*. A minority magazine, small or no, demands that enough energy should remain after one's own daily work for bread and steak, energy – but this is obvious – in keeping alive to the floating world, energy for correspondence, energy for approaching (and repelling) contributors, for the nagging pursuit of advertisements – Faber's, of course, were generous (and sensible as well) in providing some advertising revenue, and the Oxford University Press, rather surprisingly, was another generous supporter, from beginning to end, through all the six years. A minority magazine, a man-and-wife affair (though I had other helpers towards the end) needs a wet tongue for licking envelopes, not too soft a hand for tying parcels, and a sanguine expectation in one's tour of the payment-owing booksellers of Charing Cross Road and Bloomsbury.

Still, the circulation crept – at its maximum – to rather more than a thousand. The ego was succoured: the editor conceived also that he was being useful in a way that fitted his convictions. He was not simply in Fleet Street (or Tudor Street, the rather down-at-heel home of the *Morning Post* in its last years), though the curt habits of writing and subbing acquired in the quarter could appear to him to make *New Verse*, outside and between the poems, livelier and more immediate, with no cost in compromise: he was in a London, a Hampstead, this editor, which was one of art as well as letters in ferment.

It was curious to see, years after, a map in an exhibition catalogue of the fashionable Marlborough Gallery in Bond Street 'showing where some of the people connected with the modern movement in art lived in Hampstead in the 1930s', and to find on that map a blob for myself, and so for *New Verse*. Poets were around, long Norman Cameron of the party of Robert Graves, far away yet very present in the Balearic Islands, short Dylan Thomas beginning to carry his constant firkin of beer, elegant Bernard Spencer, happy-go-lucky Ruthven Todd, dark Madge, untransformed yet into a sociologist, enthusiastic Kenneth Allott (with the most beautiful of Indian or half-Indian wives) untransformed yet into a Professor of English Literature. But poets and poets perhaps mix less well than poets and painters and sculptors in a kind of cross-fertilization; in this Hampstead of the Thirties Ben Nicholson might arrive outside the door into *New Verse* conveying Braque – rather than a Warden Sparrow, if I may say so without offence – alongside him in his Austin Seven; from this Hampstead excursion might be made with the Paris studios of Mondrian or Brancusi or Mirò, descents made into private views, with their more personal evenings to follow, of new work by Moore or Nicholson; or Léger and Calder and Jean Hélion might be encountered in expeditions to John Piper's farm house outside Henley; and whenever a telegram brought the editor of *New Verse* to an obscure tea or supper with Wyndham Lewis, wasn't he, at the back of all this, meeting that first of the 'modern' artists of England, the Enemy who was also now the poet of *One Way Song*, not to say the scourge of the Sitwells and the scourge of Roger Fry and the Bloomsburies and everything which seemed, in a parasitical way, to interfere with the new objectivity? ('Why', said Picasso once to Ben Nicholson, 'when I ask about artists in England, am I always told about Duncan Grant?').

Such at any rate, though you may argue that it might have affected the result rather more, was the milieu in which *New Verse* existed. Yet one's concerns increase, leaving insufficiency of muscle for a particular concern. And insufficiency of money. I wanted to push up the number of pages – Number One had been eighteen pages, the last number in 1939 swelled to more than sixty pages – and to add illustrations, rather as if to prove to myself that I intended to continue

New Verse against a weakening impulse. (Occasionally in later years I used to dream – not the most soothing of dreams – that I had revived *New Verse*, and was licking envelopes once more). Also I was now a widower; the *Morning Post* had been closed down, there was no longer that weekly taxi full of review books to sell for half price and pay the printer. When I made a whip-round for money for *New Verse* at this time the most generous contribution, by the way, was that Wallace Stevens, whom *New Verse* had once referred to as a stuffed goldfinch. I like to remember that he saw a virtue in *New Verse*.

Was there a virtue in these goings on through six years? If there was, it would be presumptuous were I to be too complacent or pleased or eloquent about it. The tone of *New Verse* now and then, strictly the tone, I regret. I see that its existence helped a number of contributors to find themselves. I shall recall Wystan Auden's brief poem to *The Orators*,

> *Private faces in public places*
> *Are wiser and nicer*
> *Than public faces in private places.*

Also a 'Topical Note' printed in the last number but two, in the crisis autumn of 1938. 'Poetry', I wrote, 'had its finger in the crisis. When Mr Chamberlain took to his aeroplane, Masefield, who should know better, sent a stanza to the *Times* congratulating him on saving the lives of the young men. On September 26th, the Monday, the *Times* had a leader, *Poets and the Crisis:* "At moments like this it is especially fitting that we should" – here the learned and sententious ape put on a far-away look – "pay homage to poets – not for their own sakes (they are already sufficiently blessed 'in their magic robe, their burning crown', but for the sake of that clearer vision . . . " and so on. Then in that Flashing Stream, the *Times Literary Supplement*, our friend Blunden had his crisis poem when all was over. In the next week's issue it was translated into Latin.'

How many public faces there were mouthing magic robes and burning crowns in every place, exalting *The Testament of Beauty* at the expense of *The Waste Land*. How particularly at that time 'praises of the unworthy', in Coleridge's phrase, were 'felt by ardent minds as robberies of the deserving!'

Gavin Ewart, years before, in his witty, precociously able 'Phallus in Wonderland', which was so mocked by the future Warden of All Souls, had made one speaker, the 'Poet of the Generation' maintain

> *We are swept away by a strange tide,*
> *Did Mr Eliot at Hyde*
> *Park Corner in 1917 boarding a bus*
> *Foresee it? He was not born in us*
>
> *But we in him.*
> *He gave us a voice, strengthened each limb,*
> *Set us a few mental exercises*
> *And left us to our own devices.*
>
> *At first we ran up trees in distraction,*
> *Mimicked his every action,*
> *But now we are back on earth again*
> *Sheltered by a gourd and sane.*

Back on earth again. If you read through the thirty-four numbers of *New Verse* I believe you will find a fairly pronounced, if wavering, development of what I have called its 'perceptive' principles, of concern for poems of the vivid consequence.

In one late number of *New Verse* I quoted Coleridge (it was something of a personal comfort, by the way that Coleridge had been a contributor to that *Morning Post* which I worked for rather shame-facedly) on one of his contemporaries. 'A plant,' he wrote,

'sown and reared in a hot-house, for whom the very air that surrounded him had been regulated by the thermometer of previous purpose; to whom the light of nature had penetrated only through glasses and covers; who had had the sun without the breeze, whom no storm had shaken; on whom no rain had pattered; on whom the dews of heaven had not fallen! A being who had no spontaneous feeling connected with man or nature, no spontaneous impulses, no unbiased and desultory studies, no genuine science, nothing that constitutes individuality in intellect, nothing that teaches brother-hood in affection! Such was the man – such and so denaturalized the spirit on whose wisdom and philanthropy the lives and living enjoyments of so many millions of human beings was made unavoidably dependent.'

Coleridge was speaking of Pitt, of a politician, not a poet, but how it seemed to me that most of the passage could stand then for every variety, 'modernistic' or conventional, of denaturalized poet (Edith Sitwell for me).

I am not sure how much this groped-for editorial attitude manifested itself to the poets who contributed to *New Verse*, but at any rate those major contributors, still unforgotten, went on contributing faithfully from the early numbers to the last. I risk the conviction, for sure, that *New Verse* assisted a reformation for which the Thirties will be remembered and valued; and looking back I also suppose that the timing and history of *New Verse* exhibit the circumstances which justify a minority magazine: there must be a confrontation of proposition and opposition, there must be impatience with an old mode, a bad mode still powerful and damaging.

7 – ZWEMMER'S

Cézanne died in 1906. In 1921, eleven years after the Post-Impressionist exhibition in London at the Grafton Galleries, Henry Moore came from Leeds to London with a studentship at the Royal College of Art. Could he have bought a book on Cézanne anywhere in London?

Not easily. Or not at all. Kenneth Clark has written that if you hadn't seen that famous exhibition, you probably knew next to nothing of the great nineteenth-century French painters. Few people in England had seen even a reproduction of a Renoir or a Cézanne. There were no colour reproductions – if any reproductions at all? – to be had of Van Gogh. And then, in or about that year of Henry Moore's arrival in London, there did appear in the window of a newly acquired bookshop in Charing Cross Road, the booksellers' street, what the typographer Stanley Morison was to describe as 'a modest contemporary introduction' – imported – 'to the life and work of Cézanne'.

There we are back at the beginnings of the shop which came quickly to be known as Zwemmer's, and here I am, quoting Clark and Henry Moore and Morison – quoting from the tributes assembled in 1962 for Anton Zwemmer's seventieth birthday and the fortieth anniversary of the founding of the shop.

Moore wrote that this Dutch bookseller in the barren heart of London was one of the eight or nine individuals – artists apart – whose vision and vitality 'helped to change the whole climate of the English art world'. Zwemmer's was – is, because it endures – about half way between the British Museum and the National Gallery, two foci of Henry Moore's daily life. If he couldn't afford some book or other, he could look at it again and again at Zwemmer's and then walk out without buying anything. 'But nobody bothered.'

Zwemmer's was necessary – and dangerous too, because you might turn round in its narrow space between shelf and table and find yourself next to an enemy who had sneered at you in public or written a malign review of your latest book. I once turned round like that in Zwemmer's and found myself nearly treading on a rich, peppery little amateur writer on art, Tom Balston, who thought I had written a malign review of his book about John Martin – Mad Martin. I called it a silly book, and here was I squashed inescapably and accidentally against the author, who would have hit me with his silver-topped cane if his arm had not been so jammed by other customers.

Still, I cannot imagine the Twenties, the Thirties, the early Forties without Zwemmer's, I cannot imagine the inside, so cramped, so crowded with the products of every European art publisher, without Zwemmer himself suddenly appearing and towering above his customers. So I shall excerpt my own tribute from that pamphlet of tributes. Don't think its opening too histrionic, or too formal. It was meant, every word of it.

'Accept,' I wrote,

'dear Zwemmer (signing always the picture of your great bookshop, you have never needed initials), the congratulations and thanks of this individual customer; which thanks are only part of the gratitude of a generation, or several generations. For us who were young in the twenties and thirties Zwemmer's was all that the rest of London was not, was all that contradicted the stuffy philistine myopic remainder for which modernism was no more than the New English Art Club or the roofy Mediterranean canvases of the London Group. Zwemmer's was where we bought *Cahiers d'Art*, Zwemmer's was where we discovered copies of *Blast* and *The Enemy*, Zwemmer's whether we bought or not, allowed us into a various world of Ensor or de Chirico, of Klee or Picasso, aligning these masters with the masters of all past ages, Zwemmer's was the one shop where the new and lively poetry and fiction were always in stock, Zwemmer's was the rendezvous of painters, poets, novelists, the real ones, not the academic shams; and over Zwemmer's, in narrower confines than those of today's shop, between the latest *Cahier d'Art* and the enviable but hopelessly expensive monograph on the shelves, stood yourself, hands in coat pockets, immaculate, rising on your toes, a trifle sardonic, amused, diffident, helpful, knowledgeable, self-certain, unique, the great bookseller whose seventieth birthday we are celebrating. If we owed you money, we tried to avoid your eye. But I recall no bad feelings on that score. And now I know that any proper account of modernism in England, of the return of the English mind from a self-satisfied Edwardian insularity, must say more than a little of the bookshop you created, and made into a world bookshop, and of yourself. The truth is that we are in your debt beyond the chance of repayment.'

Not the first Dutchman, or Dutchman and European, to come over and teach us something about the arts, Zwemmer had arrived from Haarlem, where he was born, or rather from Amsterdam, where he had found his employment in bookselling as long ago as 1914, he stayed, he worked for Simpkin and Marshall, he worked in Charing Cross Road in a small, once famous shop – No. 78 – belonging to the philological and linguistic bookseller, Richard Jäschke. Before very long Jäschke moved out, changing premises, and Zwemmer moved in, continuing at first, though, with other general books, the sale of philology and linguistics.

John Piper, another habitué of Zwemmer's, and another of the tributeers in that pamphlet, wrote of the immense excitement, when he too was an art student, of visiting the shop (and looking at what he couldn't afford to buy). He too wrote of Zwemmer's concern and kindness. He and his wife Myfanwy started an art review, *Axis*, on less than a shoestring. Zwemmer knew about starting art magazines on a shoestring, having had a hand in the launching of one sumptuous art magazine and art publication after another, such as *Minotaure*. He and his fellow venturers weren't wealthy, but they were professionals as well as enthusiasts for the modern arts; and they had taken risks. John and Myfanwy asked Zwemmer – by this time art dealer as well as bookseller – to lend them a Picasso, 'a woman's head of the black-stained-glass-line period', which they wanted to reproduce on the cover of *Axis*. The loan would save them money. Zwemmer sympathized, and lent them the Picasso for a week, and John cut blocks of it on hard rubber plates.

Zwemmer's was for years a necessity of the time, one art professor even spoke of it as a necessary forerunner to the Courtauld Institute of Art, though I wouldn't say that bolstering art history was Anton Zwemmer's sublimest function.

There was another bookseller who did much to lighten existence in the Thirties, but one of whom publishers did not at all approve, Gaston, the king of the review booksellers. Those of us who were 'poets and hacks' (poet and hack was Betjeman's description of himself in *Who's Who*, with a trifle too much modesty perhaps or too much humility) needed to sell books sent to us to review, which we could excuse since for the most part they were books we did not want, so 'review booksellers' came into being, paying each of us reviewers half the published price for books which they in turn sold for three-quarters of the price to public libraries. They took everything in those days, good and ridiculous, learned and books which were beginning to be called 'coffee-table'. The publishers hated them, but what could they do? So that the libraries would not buy they tried perforating the flyleaf of each book with the words REVIEW COPY. They tried stamping them with the indelible blue words REVIEW COPY. Then they reflected that reviews were – as a rule – an advertising service for which they did not have to pay. Reviewers and such as Gaston were left in peace.

Was T. J. Gaston, in his office block in the Strand, that review bookseller's real name? I never discovered. He was an amiable man, glad to be a help to poets and hacks, who might in fact, though I do not think he cared one way or another, be authors of distinction. With a smile on a round face he took the books and peeled out the pound notes, if the reviewer had brought in a sufficiency of titles.

What we average poets and hacks envied were the hacks of substance, the hacks who were literary editors with an inexhaustible supply of this fodder. Thomas J. Gaston would fetch their offerings in a car. I never quite graduated to that class, even when I had my finger on the surplus review books which had come into the *Morning*

Post. Sometimes quite late I would take my review books from my basement quarters off Tudor Street down to the Strand, where Thomas J. Gaston would be waiting, after which I would take another cab up to the brasserie of the Café Royal for a late supper of chicken livers and scrambled eggs and a Mont Blanc with whoever was there for literary gossip.

At times in Hampstead, in Keats Grove, I would catch an envied sight of Gaston's van waiting outside my neighbour's, that neighbour being a much larger scale hack and reviewer than myself, the essayist, journalist and Fleet Street man Robert Lynd.

It was a charming house he lived in, but one I never regarded with much pleasure. His wife was Sylvia Lynd, a now forgotten poetess of no ability who contributed to anthologies and wrote articles in the liberal dailies which published her husband's essays in that essay age. 'I met your neighbour last night,' said Wyndham Lewis one day. 'She said you were a red-headed Jew, and stuck pins into your baby who is always screaming in the garden.'

Wasn't it at a dinner next door at the Lynds that Leonard Woolf picked up the lacy end of Sylvia Lynd's petticoat and laid it on her lap thinking it was her napkin, and Virginia Woolf, inky from a late printing session at their Hogarth Press, questioned a not very prepossessing Irish novelist about something she thought he was saying about the Holy Ghost, and he replied that what he was talking about was 'the whole East Coast'?

8 – RUTHVEN TODD

Once long, long ago, General Sir James Edmonds, historian of the First World War, sent his daughter out of his dining-room in Evelyn Gardens so that he could safely announce to her two male undergraduate friends that Field Marshal Robertson could never enter the company of a politician without getting an erection; after which she came back to serve the sweets. Her father thought – and rightly no doubt – that a well-bred girl at Lady Margaret Hall had in those days never heard the word erection except as a building term, and wouldn't have known what it meant. He explained, with some contempt and bitterness, that Field-Marshal Robertson was one of those characters who always want to be what they are not, no matter how distinguished they are. They have dream egos.

Every literary movement nourishes a character or two of this kind, in its smaller way. Every such movement has its – as a rule harmless or not very harmful – parasites, ecto-parasites, unhappy to be on the outside, and never real, on the inside. Sometimes they are innocents, sometimes rather knowing adventurers. The two most curious I have encountered were the Cingalese Tambimuttu, who was less able than most to tell a good poet from a ridiculous or bad poet, a good poem from a bad one in a current fashion, and the Scot from Edinburgh, Ruthven Todd. Tambimuttu attached himself to the neo-romanticism of Dylan Thomas and, more sensibly, to the high-rising balloon of Henry Moore. Kenneth Clark, who felt, not without reason, that he, and no other, had launched Henry on the high currents of world fame, did not like the way this odd little intruder impinged, so to say, on his property. 'What's the fellow's name? What's his name – Ramadan?'

Those who never encountered Ruthven, who suffered from an immense infection of fairly empty and thin *cacoethes scribendi*, will find a poem or two by him in anthologies, official or semi-official Scotch anthologies. They will find him, too, in the purlieus of scholarship. Among poets of the past Blake was his man – and Blake, to be sure, does attract a scholarly pseudoism, a scholarly parasitism.

He began – away from Edinburgh, where his father had been a distinguished architect who drank away his practice – with humble enough attachments, his nose nevertheless to the ground.

One day our au-pair girl in Keats Grove answered the door bell and came back from an unexpectedly long, just audible monologue on the doorstep to announce that there was a rather frightened-looking person 'who talked on and on like water running from the bath', and wanted to see the editor of *New Verse*.

Ruthven, unemployable, persistent, rather squalid-looking Ruthven, tall and somehow loose of body, came in, and didn't leave, he talked, he did not pause, and still he talked.

About nothing? So it seemed. He deceived everyone, or nearly everyone, and never meant to deceive anyone. He attached himself as a kind of temporary limpet, or slow-moving crustacean to the habitués of a bookshop in Parton Street, at the corner of Red Lion Square, whose vague proprieter, withered in one arm, had a modicum of monetary independence, which enabled him to publish Dylan Thomas's first collection of poems (but not always to pay for the copies of *New Verse* he sold). Across the road from this bookshop was a café which served excellent pastries and (very rare in London of the Thirties) drinkable coffee. It was the haunt of Dylanites and Barkerites and parasites, perching on its high stools at all times of day, when they were sufficiently in command of cash.

How did this Ruthven, this always unhealthy-looking grey oddity, keep alive? That was something of an enigma the answer to which, in part, is that he stole, a thief, an innocent, honest literary thief. He wouldn't have picked your pocket or burgled. Books and manuscripts were his game, not from shops, but from friends or those who befriended him.

He once had in his possession a copy of Louis MacNeice's *Blind Fireworks*, his first book of poems, on the blank pages of which Louis had written a long, emotional dedication to his Jewish wife Mariette (who by this time had run off with a Rhodes Scholar, a boxer, an American footballer, whom the MacNeices had befriended and taken into their house). Nothing could have been more private than that copy of *Blind Fireworks*. Louis could never have given it away, so Ruthven – Ruthv, pronounced *Riv* for short – must have sneaked it off Louis's bookshelves. No, he wasn't secretive about it. He showed it to me, a treasure, acquired by the Ecto-parasite, by this Innocent Thief, whom none of us would ever have thought of prosecuting.

How would a magistrate have lectured a vague, squalid seeming, cowering Ruthven from the bench? And I wonder where that book is now, in what private collection, in what university library, in America, in the rare books department?

Friends took Ruthven in sometimes, and resolutely cleaned him up. Women took pity on him, slept with him, even married him, found him impossible and abandoned him. There was a time when Ruthven seemed farther down and out than usual. My wife and I (we were living then not in Keats Grove, but, more cheaply, in Wildwood Terrace on the edge of Hampstead Heath) gave him a room for some weeks, a room and his meals. Ruthven owned only a single coat, filthy, and with bulging pockets. My wife thought she must have it rapidly dry-cleaned. She emptied the pockets, spread the contents on our large round table, and photographed them. What they didn't contain was any money. Ruthven did at the time earn a very little by reviewing books, enough, we thought, to make us a token payment of ten shillings a week, for the sake of his *amour propre*. He paid up, regularly. Then a bookseller whose shop I frequented in Cecil Court, one of the alleys off Charing Cross Road, told me he had just bought ten shillings' worth of books in one of which was a letter addressed to me. I was in that shop again some weeks later: the bookseller had bought more books – always ten shillings' worth or thereabouts – from the same seller, in one of which this time was my signature, and the seller was – Ruthven Todd.

Between us we kept the arrangement operating for some time. Ruthven bought the books to Cecil Court, the bookseller paid him the required ten shillings. Ruthven with scrupulous regularity paid the ten shillings to my wife, and I went down to Cecil Court, and retrieved the books, for ten shillings. What Ruthven did was to select the right number of books from high-up shelves in our sitting-room – books whose disappearance we were not likely to notice.

We never taxed the Innocent Thief with his theft, this generous creature who seldom came to see us without some present, paid for God knows how, for the children.

Ruthven aspired higher, before long, than Parton Street and Meg's Café, and Dylan Thomas and *New Verse*, and Louis MacNeice. Paris beckoned to him, and New York. He frequented studios in Paris, he made friends – if that is exactly the right word, with Miró, who painted him a startling crimson watercolour inscribed *Pour Ruthven Todd – Miró*, he took money and more money from foundations – how could they have been gulled so easily? – for work he never carried out, or through. He graduated eventually to the meinie of Robert Graves in Majorca, where he died, an innocent than whom, to borrow Crabbe's words about his vicar, none

> *left this world of sin*
> *More like the being that he entered in.*

9 – TWO OXFORD POETS

Looking across the years, which are so close and yet stretch back so far, nothing seems to me more extraordinary, whatever it can be put down to, perhaps only accident, only coincidence, than the sudden efflorescence of Oxford poets in the Thirties and the early Forties. There they were, Auden, MacNeice, Clere Parsons, Norman Cameron, Bernard Spencer, Stephen Spender, Cecil Day Lewis, and one or two women poets as well, notably Joy Scovell, one of those modest poets who have never advanced or been pushed from shyness into the celebrity they deserved.

Middle-class – yes, most of them came from – perhaps I had better say most of them occurred in – educated families of the professional middle class, children of the clergy, of doctors, civil servants. They went to the maligned class of public schools, the middle class of those middle-class institutions, rather than the grander schools attractive to the aristocracy and the rich. Few, if any, of those schools actively discouraged learning. They had their sixth forms; somewhere or other on the premises, their authorities inscribed a Gloria Domus, listing scholarships and university honours. They maintained their cricket elevens, their Rugby fifteens, their OTCs, which being interpreted meant their *Officers* Training Corps, in case of need – need, as it proved, against the Germans, in the stinking mud and savagery of Flanders (where two brothers of mine found their death), and in the Royal and Genteel Navy. Let no one with the wrong accent apply, at least with much hope.

Among the boys there were bullies, hearties, arm-twisters, and often dull heroes of the playing field.

There were also aesthetes, who survived. Among the masters there were thugs, dull persons, strong-armed and adept with the cane, which they were encouraged to use.

Civilized parents were aware of all this, but regarded the

47

'strengthening process' as worthwhile, worth the school fees, necessary for the future welfare of their children (on the whole, let the girl children go hang, and get married, their manners and their accents being correct). Anyhow, were there not two universities for their children to go to, in eventual escape, on their way, if luck went with them, to high office in church and government? It is true that escape might continue to be a necessity now and then. 'Hearties' also lurked in the two universities, they might have rooms on your staircase, and they did occasionally get out of hand. For instance, at Oxford Bernard Spencer, a slight almost girlish creature not to be found, I think, or imagined, squelching in the mud under a pack of Rugby forwards, grew side-whiskers which the hearties of his college forcibly removed. Louis MacNeice and some of his friends suffered occasional trouble, debagging and room-wrecking and the like, Louis getting his own back in a poem about the ringleader, the Honourable John Stanley, Eton and Balliol, which won't be found in his *Collected Poems*, though it deserves its corner. It ran like this,

> *God is complaining*
> *Of our Honourable Stanley.*
> *It doesn't stop raining,*
> *God is complaining.*
> *He rows without training*
> *Because he's so manly.*
> *God is complaining*
> *Of the Honourable Stanley.*

Yet still childish hearties like our Honourable Stanley could be circumvented and avoided for the most part, and ridiculed, though drink might always set them off; moreover general opinion and sympathy were not on their side.

An Irish – or Anglo-Irish – gentleman, such as Louis MacNeice's father, Protestant rector and bishop to be, knew better than to leave his son to Irish schools and schoolmasters. He needed to cross the sea, and be prepared in an English preparatory school for an English public school which would rid that diffident child, of whom I shall have more to say, from all sorts of marginal, provincial faults and fit him into multinationality and entire respectability no less than an Englishman born. My own parent, an elderly clergyman who had seven children by a third wife, had himself gone to Cambridge by way of an old monastic foundation, a monastic grammar school, which in his childhood had still been regarded as second to few schools in England for its scholarship. But times having changed, he too felt the need, fees or no, to send his children to what he no doubt considered as the still novel public schools, which would be their route to a high rank in the services, a knighthood or an Indian governorship, or – who knows? – a bishopric or a good living in a parsonage more comfortable than his own, or a fellowship of the Royal Society. Only the First World War, then the Second, spoilt those hopes, at least to some degree.

Most of what I have just written applies to that Oxford poet, Bernard Spencer, another elegant Marlburian, who was to die, a little mysteriously as it turned out, in the elegant gentlemanly service of the British Council, and who went from Marlborough to Corpus Christi College, of which his Spencer uncle was bursar, a gentleman in the gentleman's profession of managing estates.

Bernard was not in fact, of middle-class keepings, or at least of middle-class descent. He came of the great family of the Spencers of Althorpe and the Spencer earls, which would not, I suppose, have endeared him to labourite intellectuals, or to many of the poetasters of more recent years. To him this aristocratic affiliation made not the smallest difference. He gave no sign of it. I knew nothing of it until years after, and then only discovered it by accident. He seemed content to be his private self, without much in the way of public reputation. He wrote his poems and did not push himself as a writer. I put this down to rather low pressure of being. But there he was, in himself beautiful, and easygoing, married to a girl, an Irish actress, no less beautiful than himself, though more amused by existence – not an actress of much talent. This Norah Spencer lives and has her appearance in one of the more – no, in the most delightful of his poems, by way of which I am reminded of her whenever I buy red tulips in the spring and set them on mid-table in a green jug.

> *When she carries food to the table and stoops down*
> *– Doing this out of love – and lays soup with its good*
> *Tickling smell, or fry winking from the fire*
> *And I look up, perhaps from a book I am reading*
> *Or other work: there is an importance of beauty*
> *Which can't be accounted for by there and then,*
> *And attacks me, but not separately from the welcome*
> *Of the food, or the grace of her arms.*
>
> *When she puts a sheaf of tulips in a jug*
> *And pours in water and presses to one side*
> *The upright stems and leaves that you hear creak,*
> *Or loosens them, or holds them up to show me,*
> *So that I see the tangle of their necks and cups*
> *With curls of her hair, and the body they are held*
> *Against, and the stalk of the small waist rising*
> *And flowering in the shape of breasts;*
>
> *Whether in the bringing of the flowers or the food*
> *She offers plenty, and is part of plenty,*
> *And whether I see her stooping, or leaning with the flowers,*
> *What she does is ages old, and she is not simply,*
> *No, but lovely in that way.*

'Part of Plenty' was the name which he gave to that poem, and I reprint it here, after having been perhaps the second or the third person ever to read it, in a certainty that it should be better known, Bernard Spencer not being a poet, to much extent, of the anthologies.

The flat which she and Bernard made for themselves in St John's Wood matched both the tulips and themselves, matched Norah's tulip grace and tulip sinuosity and tulip freshness. The curtains, the decorations, the carpets, the furniture in their flat combined comfort and harmony and artificiality to a degree I have never seen equalled.

I would say that another characteristic of their flat and themselves was a lively innocence. So they died young.

It was an experience, almost a trial, to walk anywhere with Norah, of course in London, in Central London, or suburban London, not in the country, to which they didn't belong. Everyone turned round at her beauty – she was nicely conscious of it – and at the startling, extra-fashionable eccentricity of her dress. Sitting opposite Norah in the tube one evening, a drunk man noticed her, noticed her nylon or silken legs, and her knees (skirts were not worn very high at that time, or not as high as Norah wore them). He imitated her, he bared his hairy bony knees, he put his feet together, lifted up his heels to the same height, in mimicry, which everyone in the carriage enjoyed, including Norah. I see her now, if a little embarrassed, amused, raising her eyebrows, while the tube went on and on.

She told a story about her own beauty *vis-à-vis* Bernard's beauty. Going out to Salonika where Bernard was working on English teaching and the like for the British Council, she was noticed – very distinctly and admiringly noticed, morning in, morning out, when she went shopping, by a Greek policeman on traffic control, whose male beauty almost equalled that of Bernard. 'Come and see my policeman,' she said to Bernard when he was taking time off on a first Saturday morning. 'He makes wonderful eyes at me.' They went together – and the policeman made wonderful eyes at Bernard.

How did she die so young? I am not sure, though I have been told that, like my own first wife, she succumbed to tuberculosis, in that appalling disease's last decade or so as a killer, so often a killer of young women.

Bernard married again, and had a son; and then somehow – we had lost all touch with one another – fell from a train in Vienna, in 1963. He was fifty-three, which I find it hard to credit, he and Norah, now so long dead, existing for me still as permanent images of youth.

Was Bernard a good poet, even much of a poet? I cannot pretend that he was. He had been associated one way and another with the Oxford poets, and the Marlborough poets, and with the Cairo and

North African poets who served in the desert campaigns. But I say that he wrote, he was forced into writing, one good poem, that 'Part of Plenty,' into the words and cadence and vision of which he translated his young wife. Good poems – especially good lyrical poems or emotional poems about love and beauty – become a part of their readers, as that 'Part of Plenty', that major part of the plenty he enjoyed even to the creak of tulip stems, long ago became a part of me – and would have done, whether I had or hadn't known of the existence and nature of Norah Spencer. 'Lovers, we had our share of the ideal.'

He wrote touchingly of the dying of his father, once more a rare adequate stimulus –

> *The old man bearded with illness weakens upstairs.*

He wrote well against greed, oppression, misery and poverty:

> *The poor were shunted nearer to beasts. The cops recruited.*
> *The rich became a foreign community. Up there leapt*
> *Quiet folk gone nasty,*
> *Quite strangely distorted, like a photograph that has slipped.*
>
> *Hearing the drunken roars of Money from down the street,*
> *'What is to become of us?' the people in bed would cry:*
> *And oh, the thought strikes chill:*
> *What's to become of the world if Money should suddenly die?*
>
> *Should suddenly take a toss and go down crack on his head?*
> *If the dance suddenly finished, if they stopped the runaway bus,*
> *If the trees stopped racing away?*
> *If our hopes come true and he dies, what's to become of us?*
>
> *Shall we recognize each other, crowding around the body?*
> *And as we go stealing off in search of the town we have known*
> *– What a job for the Sanitary Officials;*
> *The sprawled body of Money, dead, stinking, alone!*

'Part of Plenty' (1937) and the poem about his father on his death bed I am pleased to have published in *New Verse*.

Norah and Bernard, I must not forget to say, were given to romantic scheming for the happiness of their friends. They had more than a finger in the first marriage of Ruthven Todd to a tiny Scots wife from Edinburgh. It wasn't what they hoped it would be, that marriage. They nursed another plan when my first wife died and left me with a child. I was to marry a dark handsome girl, an Edinburgh friend of theirs, who wanted a child, but had had her womb removed. I am not sure we were either of us consulted. But when I did marry again Norah considered it a duty to take my very young Austrian girl, who had come from Salzburg, round the smarter London shops, and fit her with pocket Venus garments nearly as charmingly outrageous as the clothes she wore herself, and to parade her in front of mirrors trying on small saucy hats of black velvet from which there depended black veils with pink spots.

That, too, wasn't quite as acceptable as Norah hoped in the gay kindliness of her heart.

An unknowing backward look at the Oxford of the various poets around the Bernard Spencer's time might suppose or suspect that the homosexuality of several of them was an element in the way they came together, and a reason why, incidentally, women poets were so little to the fore.

It would be a wrong suspicion; or one only of being smart after the events; and were I to ask myself why, for instance, an Oxford poet who has written early and late with strong tenderness such as Joy Scovell isn't better known or known as she deserves to be, I have to answer because she was a woman less concerned with celebrity and self-importance than with what she discovered in being alive, and in love.

If she reads this, and finds what I say a little impertinent, reflecting that I met her only once, in her Oxford nursery, as she was putting her children to bed, I shall reply that I have always been conscious of her as a poet; and that I have one special thing to recall about her poems and herself. She began certainly with that same middle-class education which helped to form other Oxford poets, on the Westmorland fells at Casterton, a modest star, held up to later generations of the sixth form, of the Clergy Daughter's School made both famous and infamous by having harboured the Brontë girls so grimly. She too found herself at Casterton as the daughter of a clergyman of the Church of England.

When I thrust myself towards her in admiration (undergraduate poetry days were long over) it was partly because I wanted to include in a radio programme some poems from her first book, *Shadows of Chrysanthemums* (1944), a late-coming book among Oxford poetry, seeing that Joy Scovell was born in 1907, which was also the year in which Auden and MacNeice were born (Bernard Spencer was two years younger).

She said no, a firm no, to the broadcasting of one poem, 'A Betrothal', which is a love poem, as love poems should be, of particular loveliness. It might be printed, yes, but it was too intimate, too much an act of herself, in her own voice, to be broadcast. Or that is how I interpreted that resolute refusal. Ten years before she had been married, this quiet girl of the Thirties, to a husband of great distinction, the zoologist Charles Elton, Director of the Bureau of Animal Population, and an FRS to be. I have described her poems as loving poems, pure, alert and fastidious – 'of a kind which is always uncommon and very easily disregarded'; and by reason of one poem, 'Orchids in a Drought', the first Early Purple Orchids of the year, of the full spring, the early summer, are flowers I associate with Joy Scovell's poems.

Not long ago I read some more than usually foolish generalizing comments on 'poetry of the Thirties' as if it were all of a piece, or as if the comments were adequate description of any of it. The professional commentator wrote of 'the pansy falderols of the Thirties'. Then he had the additional nerve to echo that recent poetry about deprivation and decay was preferable to Wordsworth on daffodils; comment of a kind which isn't going to lead his students to the poems of Joy Scovell – to Joy Scovell beginning a poem

> *I saw my love, younger than primroses,*
> *Sleeping in a wood*

or writing again of that husband of hers crouching among flowers
and grass,

> *thigh-deep, a patient man in flannels,*
> *With his grass-green net still, and in repose*
> *His heavy thoughtful head,*

who

> *seemed rooted in the brome,*
> *Stock of that natural garden, never so at home.*

10 — HERBERT READ

Hampstead in the Thirties was not an expensive place to live. It had its big houses for sure, its grand houses, but within easy distance of the tube station and the bus terminal plenty of Regency corners and little villa houses falling into shabbiness or decay and costing little to rent (or buy if you had the money). This high district was full of artists and writers of an older generation. Paul Nash lived (but rather well) in a biggish Edwardian house on Haverstock Hill. Orage, sunk now, I suppose, to an inhabitant only of other men's biographies and memoirs, fixed friends with his sharp eyes as they passed his garden gate at the bottom of Keats Grove. Higher up in John Street Edwin Muir was visible through cracked and unpainted French window frames, midnight after midnight, thumping out badly paid translations on a typewriter which seemed nearly as broken as the house. On a late tube as likely as not Charles Ginner was to be encountered, coming come from an evening in the Café Royal, cherubic, deaf and jolly, for ever finding something to laugh about. And so on, left, right and centre. Auden and Isherwood reported that they once went into the *pissoir* attached to the public house in the Vale of Health, and surprised an elderly author with a white beard writing up 'I am sixteen years old and would like to meet another boy under the clock at Hampstead Tube Station . . . ' He saw them, put his pencil away and shuffled off (but how did they know he was an author?).

Younger writers and painters crowded in during the Thirties, and if there was a London centre of the new 'modernism', a centre of that centre was certainly the Mall Studio off Parkhill Road in which Herbert Read and his new, Edinburgh wife lived next door to the white studio, the white interior alongside, occupied, in hygienic, but gay clarity, by Ben Nicholson and Barbara Hepworth.

The Reads were hospitable to a degree. Their studio home was a place of parties, of extraordinary entertainment. It was where

56

nationalities and generations mixed (with a notable absence, though, of Auden and his closer friends). Braque might be there, or Jean Hélion, from Paris, or Eliot gayer than his reputation, actually singing 'Frankie and Johnny'. The exodus from Hitler's Reich having begun, one might walk into the solemn dignified company of Gropius to find oneself face to face with slow-smiling Moholy-Nagy from the Bauhaus (furniture all round to match, as far as it could be found). Ben and Barbara from next door would be there, and the Moores from down the road, Upper Parkhill Road (the studio block the Moores lived in has been swept away). There was a game we used to play, invented by one of Henry Moore's friends, ingredients, wall-paper, unrolled and turned blank side up, drawing pins to attach the wall-paper to a long table, coloured chalks, a separate colour for each of the players, who chalked in – that was fun, and I wish a specimen or two had been preserved – something like a sixteenth-century chart, with headlands and straits and reefs and islands and whales and mermaids. In turn each player grasped his colour-identifiable chalk, and with eyes shut, started a sailing line from harbour at one end, and advanced towards the other end, trying to avoid being wrecked on one or other of the obstacles. Each player, before his turn, was allowed a long look at this gay coloured entertainingly drawn sea-course. Who were the winners, every time or nearly every time, steering a clean passage? Ben Nicholson and Henry Moore. Poets weren't dabs at visual form.

Herbert Read, a Yorkshire farmer's son, was gentle and mild and generous. He was no genius, he had no very acute perception, appreciating perception of the arts of painting, sculpture, or writing. I would even say there was something to Wyndham Lewis's charge that he had never looked a picture in the face, although he knew the kind of picture to look in the face.

He was saintly, but private saintliness does not attract public encomium. Not much of poet, to tell the truth not much of a writer, he was an art apostle who stuck to his preaching. Eliot in those Thirties was still a name to earn a sneer from right-minded men of letters and from academic authority, and as Eliot's friend and lieutenant Herbert incurred his share of the abuse.

'Do you tell us, Read, that this Picasso of yours doesn't know what his picture will be when he starts it?'

'Yes,' came Read's answer to this right-minded academic colleague at Edinburgh after one of his lectures as Edinburgh University's new Professor of Fine Art.

'Oh, well . . . ' and that was the end of the matter (and very soon came the end of Herbert's professorship).

Herbert, to be sure, was or became an introducer, an over-introducer. Around at the time in London there was a portly Hungarian, Josef Bard, married to the surrealist painter Eileen Agar, not an exile, but one of those foreigners who used to descend on the provincial but wealthy English to teach them a little about making films. In the seventeenth century they came to teach the English how to paint. He was a wit, and though a friend of Henry Moore's he knew where to be when, and he had a habit, or so it seemed, of suddenly and wittily intruding into one's life and as suddenly disappearing. He intruded one day like that in the South of France. We were staying on the Île de Port Cros, where we had a habit of going down to the harbour at midday to watch new arrivals, who often included rather bizarre unofficially honeymooning couples, who would photograph each other naked (not quite the thing to do in those days). One day I saw Eileen Agar's Hungarian stepping slowly down the gangplank. He held out his hand, and said, without preliminary, or greeting, 'Grigson, I have come from London, where a new edition of the Bible has been published with an introduction by Herbert Read.'

The contempt Herbert came in for wasn't always as mild and funny as that, but some of it was explicable, if not exactly earned or justified. For instance, when he opened the big surrealist exhibition in London in 1936, his speech began 'Ladies and gentlemen, this is an historic occasion . . . ', which was not quite the cliché for introducing Londoners to a revolutionary art movement.

Naive? No, that is not his proper epithet. Humble? That won't do either, not entirely. When he was knighted – and he deserved to be, according at least to the public canons of knighthood, no one having done more or so much to make art a living interest at last in our time for the indifferent English, there followed the usual jokes and japes, ill-humoured often about the first anarchist ever to be knighted, as if Herbert had been an old-fashioned Russian bomb-thrower. Herbert, though, felt some explanation of his acceptance would be in order to quieten the surprise of his friends. To me he said 'I didn't feel important enough to refuse.'

I owe him, I must say, rather a halcyon period of my life, my London life; that life which came to an end with the war, and so scattered the Hampstead clan, and the Hampstead promise of much greater performance.

One thing Herbert told me I must remember to include. Herbert, Bonamy Dobrée and Eliot at one time shared a flat. Eliot was inclined to sleep in, or sleep late, on Sunday mornings. Getting up as usual one Sunday, Herbert and Bonamy found Eliot wasn't there. And Eliot's bowler hat was missing from its peg. He had gone off to early morning service. It was their first sign of Eliot's active but rather secretive conversion.

Starving through the leafless wood
Trolls run scolding for their food;
And the nightingale is dumb,
And the angel will not come.

Cold, impossible, ahead
Lifts the mountain's lovely head
Whose white waterfall could bless
Travellers in their last distress.

I was not altogether clear why I went to America in the autumn of 1951, or why I was asked to go as a guest of the State Department. The drive, the need, for cultural propaganda didn't explain *me*, and I have wondered who put my name forward.

I made a vast, tiresome, tiring journey. I saw extraordinary things, of course, like a belated de Crèvecoeur seeing the novel and unfamiliar. Humming birds − Red Rubies I think they were called − hung round the still flowering fuchsia bushes, in a San Francisco park in which the grass was the greenest imaginable. Great cables, great hawsers of kelp sprawled on Pacific sand, on which there was no one but myself, frightening great hawsers −

All dripping in tangles green,
Cast up by a lonely sea,
If purer for that, O Weed,
Bitterer, too, are ye?
Herman Melville

Yes, but to be seeing, actually seeing the Pacific! Edging the other shore, Connecticut marshes were on fire in autumn leaves, Morning Glories covered a farmhouse wall, or the wall of what had once been a farmhouse before New England farmers had moved west, and abstract artists, and writers as abstract as they could be, had moved in, and skunks, those beautiful natives, had been left to play in the scrub once more.

I slightly shook the celebrated glass flowers and glass bumblebees of Harvard, which so authentically belonged to new America, and wondered at the Unicorn tapestries, at the Cloisters, in New York, which decidedly did not belong to America, but – I mean, of course, by nativity – to my own Europe.

It was the people who puzzled me, and still puzzle me, because they seemed put together, glued together, out of so many stocks. Twenty minutes of relief was sitting in a parkside church in ever-enormous New York listening to Wystan Auden mumbling through a sermon. When we went off together I dived into my bag and gave him a copy of what I think was the first book written about him, by Richard Hoggart. It had been published just before I left England.

He took it with thanks, but not much gratification, and I doubt if he ever read it. Probably he thought it not a very decent act, to read about oneself, pro or con.

How wonderful to reflect that this essentially English poet, whom I knew, though there was much to separate us or interfere with a possible intimacy, had lain on the summer grass, Vega conspicuous overhead, on the bald summit of Malvern, that mount of archaic rock from which England could be surveyed, that mount of the vision of Piers Plowman, who meant so much to this new poet, his qualities made so evident by Eliot himself, who pushed him towards us in the *Criterion*. It was in Eliot's *Criterion* that *Paid on Both Sides* first appeared, in 1930, page after page of it, and none stale or boring; and it was in the autumn of the same year that it was printed again in a thin pamphlet of poems, two years after Auden ceased to be an Oxford undergraduate. Not easily or entirely to be conveyed are the feelings spread among us by this new usage of language, by the kind of drama which seemed at work between the beginning and the ending of each new line, the import of which we may not altogether have understood, and which allowed for sneering much as Eliot's *The Waste Land* only eight years before had allowed for the inimical sneering, which still had not died away.

This kind of internal dramatic quality in Auden's verse destroyed a too familiar, too settled monotony in manner and subject, yet how English it was from the summit of Malvern, how central it quickly seemed to our history and our existence, making us feel, whatever may now be said about other happenings of the time, political and social and demoniac as well, that we had entered another world. Dark cloudage, ominous cloudage, was recognizable, yet in a new light it no longer had to be misted with complacency.

It was possible to read these poems and feel that here was a new poet for us, poised in the mid-way height, or level rather, between classes, between wealth or well-to-do-ness and poverty, culture and necessity. As in a line by Bernard Spencer we could feel that, without compromising poetry, here we were being given

> *the pride*
> *To be capable of action, to speak out plainly.*

We largely knew what threatened

> *Our freedom to lounge in the green world, to be*
> *happy beneath the*
> *Clocks of its cities.*

Here was someone newly wise and passionate who encouraged us to be on the right side, even if (from another of Bernard's poems)

> *"'What have we to live by?' beats back into*
> *brain*
> *And cannot be frowned away."*

And additionally, as a lyrically tender concomitant, we were soon given in 1933, by the same publisher, the blue-jacketed *Poems* by Stephen Spender –

> *Our goal which we compel: Man shall be man.*

But I am going too quickly from the first Auden – the first Auden I knew about, not the first Auden I knew. Even so I am far from being able to provide one of those confident surveys of the whole Land of

Auden from start to finish, beginning with that first wonderful impact.

Their contemporaries are likely to be poor guides or only partial guides to the totality of a writer they admire, to a writer whose existence in his poems comes to seem a part of that own existence. Contemporaries live most in the work they first recognize. I live – perhaps they are the best if not the most profound, profundity not being all – in the poems of the earlier books up to *New Year Letter* in 1941. I suppose that later on, when Auden embraced more –

> *How hard it is to set aside*
> *Terror, concupiscence and pride,*
> *Learn who and where and how we are,*
> *The children of a modest star,*
> *Frail, backward, clinging to the granite*
> *Skirts of a sensible old planet.*

– he no longer composed so well.

Leaving that topic, then, I can go back and back, asking how we first detect – or rather how do we so often miss – the new writer; again, though, without providing an exactly confident answer. The first poem I remember by Auden, never republished, and I have never hunted it out again, coming almost to believe that I dreamt its existence, seemed to me to have risen out of an 'Englishness' (he was English after all) until then unexpressed or not isolated in a poem. Auden was reading English; English at Oxford involved him in Old English, which involved him in *Beowulf*. In the poem he saw the blood-trail which had dripped from Grendel after his arm and shoulder had been ripped off by Beowulf. The blood shone, was phosphorescent on the grass – or so I remember the poem (in the *Cherwell* perhaps?). It was as if Auden, this untidy, untied up, short-sighted, pallid person from Christ Church, had given imaginative place and 'reality' to something exploited for the Examination Schools, yet rooted in the English origins. It was the same with many of his early poems; a measure suggesting fatality, assonances and alliterations coming together to make a new verbal actuality as it

63

might be of rock or quartz, a milieu of the profound Midlands, half aboriginal, half soiled or damaged, half abandoned; the very palpable truth of something, emotions and attitudes included, both anxieties and satisfactions, at once recognizable and pertinent, autochthonic and not provincial (though intimated a little in Housman, and more in Hardy).

In smart Oxford, and the smart Outside, a fashion then was for the frothy, vicious, aesthetic, and selfish; an aesthetical, excluding snobbery re-exhibited for us in the detestable diaries of Evelyn Waugh. The contrast. This is England, this is man: this is Us, this is our sensation. We only are. From Auden I first learnt what the trolls in *Peer Gynt* were up to, and amounted to, when they said 'To thyself be enough'; and how skilfully and suavely our trollishness disguised itself – like Auden's devil in *New Year Letter*.

Within a few years (*The Orators* and *The Dance of Death* and the first *Poems* already published) poems were coming to me from Birmingham or from the Malverns, and I was publishing them in *New Verse*. They came on half sheets of notepaper, on long sheets of lined foolscap, in that writing an airborne daddy-long-legs might have managed with one dangling leg, sometimes in pencil, sometimes smudged and still less easy to decipher. They had to be typed before they went to the printer, and in the act of typing each poem established itself. It was rather like old-fashioned developing in the dark-room, but more certain, more exciting.

> *At the far end of the enormous room,*
> *An orchestra is playing to the rich.*

– there at last on the white page, to be clearer still on the galley, was the first entire sight of a new poem joining our literature.

> *Earth has turned over; our side feels the cold . . .*

England of a new generation was beginning to widen into the world, the anxiety and the concern of the English individual, Wystan Hugh Auden, beginning to encompass the anxieties of man.

August for the people and their favourite islands . . .

Dear, though the night is gone . . .

A new poetry, poems to appear again in that wonder-book, *Look Stranger!*, in 1936.

The 'English individual' – what kind of a name was Auden? In the early Auden years I liked to think this name of his must be Old Norse, proper for a poet who knew about trolls running along the edges of the mind, liked Morris's *Sigurd the Volsung*, read the sagas, and visited (I had been there before him, impelled, I suppose, by the same kind of reading) the 'sterile, immature', cindery landscape of Icelandic dales and plains – the great plains 'forever where the cold fish is hunted'. The surname dictionary says Auden could be Anglo-Scandinavian, *Healfdene*, 'half-Dane'. That would do. But it could also be English, from *Ælfwine*, 'elf-friend'. That, too, would serve for this Wystan Auden, the elf-friend, the magician, allowing that there are good and bad elves, good and bad magicians. Others too, like myself, preferred to think of this loose-limbed blonde-haired creature we so admired as Icelandic by remote origin. Iceland was in fashion with middle-class children of Auden's kind or from rectories and vicarages. As most of us had done, I suspect Auden had read *Eric Brighteyes* by Rider Haggard, and *Grettir the Outlaw* by Baring-Gould; to which Auden would have added a saga or two in translation, as well as at any rate some of the heroic Norse or Icelandic poems by William Morris, whom he always admired. I was drawn to Morris's poem about a first louring sight of Iceland on the horizon, and had visited lava deserts and great waterfalls and farms which had been saga-steads, where the sheep-dogs which greeted you were named after the dogs in the sagas. Certainly it was no surprise that one of Auden's early journeys should be to that Iceland of his in company with Louis MacNeice.

So much for *Auden*. What about Wystan? That was another unusual name. I found that, as well as a parish called Audenshaw, in Lancashire, there was a parish in Shropshire – Auden's Shropshire of the deserted lead mines – called Wistanstow; and didn't the guidebook to Shropshire by the Reverend John Ernest Auden –

Auden's uncle, I think – relate the martyrdom of Wystan, son of Widmund, grandson of Wiglaf, King of Mercia, who wished 'to become an heir of a heavenly kingdom', not of an earthly one? Wystan's treacherous cousin – at Wistanstow – struck him down with a sword after giving him the kiss of peace. 'For thirty days a column of light extending from the spot where he was slain, was seen by all those who dwelt there, and every year on the day of his martyrdom, the hairs of his head, severed by the sword, sprang up like grass.'

Sentimental, beside any possible point, to connect the name-saint, the Half-Dane, the Elf-friend, the magician, the poet, and the poems? Well, this poet wasn't called Marmaduke Rees-Mogg, his names fitted his poems, they symbolized a depth of historical, local humus from which this poet could spread above and below ground from local into universal. For me more than a thirty days column of light stood up from his poems.

> *Intellectual disgrace*
> *Stares from every human face,*
> *And the seas of pity lie*
> *Locked and frozen in each eye.*

Picking through a folder, from these *New Verse* days, I found on the back of a sheet of *New Verse* notepaper, a statement excerpted from Auden at this early time:

'When a poet is writing verse, the feeling, as it were, excites the words and makes them fall into a definite group, going through definite movements, just as feeling excites the different members of a crowd and makes them act together. Metre is group excitement among words, a series of repeated movements. The weaker the excitement, the less words act together and upon each other.'

His feeling was already rising to its greatest power to excite. And the early article in which he wrote that, when he was twenty-five, to explain verse to children (and their parents), he called 'Writing, or the Pattern between People'. Between people – even then. Writers 'would like to be read by everybody and for ever. They feel alone, cut off from each other in an indifferent world where they do not live for very long. How can they get in touch again?'

The wish for company, the desire to make – these, he said, are the respectable reasons for writing.

He had, when he began, no doubts of his vocation; he accepted his gifts, learning and admitting as well where he was limited or fell short. His Oxford tutor, Nevill Coghill, told me once, on a night drive between Reading and Oxford during which we talked the whole way of Auden, a story which might have appalled the Auden of his middle or later understanding. As usual Coghill had interviewed his new undergraduates, and he had asked Auden his stock question, after a while:

Tutor: 'And what are you going to do, Mr Auden, when you leave the university?'

Auden: 'I am going to be a poet.'

Tutor: (since something must be said.) 'Well, in – in that case you should find it very useful to have read English.'

Auden: (after a silence). 'You don't understand, I am going to be a great poet.'

Not all of his writing – but who cares, except the pedant who hates and misunderstands both the arts and the readers he thinks he is serving? – is 'great' or free of dullness. The appalling uniqueness of each great writer includes the different proportions in him of fudge and gold. And what writer, Tolstoy, Hugo, Baudelaire, Melville, Shakespeare, is not a warning against demands for a sustained perfection in literature, as if the great writer's graph ascended steeply and at the worst flattened to a long high level? Zigzags are his condition. And Auden had to write for a living, in our indifferent Anglo-Saxony, which gets its poems but expects its poets to live on book-reviewing and the free provision of stale air.

'I am going to be a great poet' – in that early essay I mentioned, he spoke of the writer as being the soil and the gardener: 'The soil part of him does not know what is going on, the gardener part of him has learnt the routine.' Better to be a bad gardener than bad soil, he went on. His soil proved deep and extensive as the Fens. If sometimes he gardened poorer patches of himself, he was a supremely able, dedicated gardener.

Not all of his poems are kind, but most of them are, and he was – exemplifying the unshiftably true fact that the great writer is always, in the base and inside the total of himself – the good man. A book about Auden (though I cannot bear to read such books) which was sent to me from Australia, ends with a note by Rex Warner mentioning Auden's great kindliness and the way he inspired 'great affection in all who know him'. To be kind – not to be cruel – isn't to be evasive, and I see as inseparable from his kindliness Auden's much debated Christianity. It has upset old faithfuls, it repels new readers. For me it demands too much of an 'as if' for intellectual assent; but I see it as wrung from Auden by his long look at the muddle, wickedness, goodness, and necessities of man; wrung from him by desperation about ourselves; not as back-sliding, not as a contradiction, but as an enlargement, accepted or no, of his first, limited Marxist cures for our discontent.

Aren't poets, in one form or another, naturally religious men, or nothing? His Christianity may not be what we want, it may disappoint us, it may not be what we suppose is most effective, or most enjoyable; but is it discreditable for a poet to find himself – allowing this to have been Auden's location – outside and beyond poetry in the end?

What Auden doesn't do is opt either from us or from our primary world. I see that is why he turned from, rather than against, Hardy. When old, Hardy wrote, in strict continuation, that he had not cared for life, but that since life had cared for him he owed it some loyalty; which must have seemed grudging, and more than half defeated. It was unkindliness – unkindliness to man, who has to live, and in this world. The unevasive Auden I revere and love, conceived, like Pasternak, that we are guests of existence, which must be honoured

68

with delight. If that is one reason why he has been a rhythm and a revolving or shifting fixture in our lives, I shall insist that Auden's Lond Mynd and Malverns became the hills of the world. He saw man and the world as Langland saw them from the Malverns.

Our English fortune is to share peculiarities with him, as Americans share them with Whitman or Russians with Pasternak, or the French with Hugo. He is for everyone, for us he is extra, by language, by keepings and milieu. In *A Certain World*, which he published in 1970 (and which by dedication was my ultimate gift from Auden), I was delighted to encounter so much, so late in him, of our primary world, whether, with everything else, in extracts from Cobbett, a winter and mountain poem by an Irishman of the tenth century, or a poem on roads by Edward Thomas. Who else would have known, say, about Ivor Gurney making delight of the world, in his distress, out of the Malverns or the Cotswolds:

Cotswold's farther early Italian Blue arrangement . . .

Up in the air there beech tangles wildly in the wind.

If we follow him round, as he celebrates, investigates, discards, adds, re-attempts, we find in him, I declare, explicit recipes for being human. And implicit ones, in poems, stanzas, lines, again and again, which give us in sonority and movement the additional bonus of what their language cannot say – the bonus of great poetry.

The last time I sat at a table with Auden was not so long before his death. We had lunch with him at Stephen Spender's house in St John's Wood. When we rang the bell the door was opened in what I would call rather a fluffy or shuffly way by Auden – Auden of the furrowed face, who spoke immediately, wasting no time in greeting or enquiry, but holding an object out, a book, and saying 'Here's a book I've dedicated to you.' Eliot was dead by that time, and besides my wife, Jane Grigson, and myself the third guest was Eliot's widow Valerie Eliot, wearing emeralds and splendidly, tightly filling an emerald dress. Decades sat together round the dining-room table, Wystan, still wearing those soft slippers, not drunk but slightly whisky-blurred, in speech, not in mind or spirit, directing all we talked about and keeping Stephen Spender in place, contradicting him now and then a little brusquely. After coffee, after brandy, and another brandy, he bore that channelled heavy face of his off to sleep.

One thing I learnt that day was how much Wystan liked food. I don't mean that he was greedy, that he wolfed all that came on his plate, but that he spoke of food as something, since it was our substance in a way, to be properly prepared, properly treated, properly valued as an element of civilization and culture. So after his death I was delighted, but not altogether surprised, to find him talking in praise and in fun (in his antimasque *The Entertainment of the Senses*, which was his last piece of writing for the stage, a collaboration with Chester Kallman) of

Dear Elizabeth David and darling Jane Grigson.

The difference in that food compliment, that passing benison on the art of preparing food and not taking it all out of tins, was, I think, that he had only read Elizabeth's books and not used them, whereas he had read and used my wife's books, and now came face to face with her on that late occasion in St John's Wood. (M. F. K. Fisher was another cookery writer – see Auden's 'To-night at Seven-Thirty' – whom Wystan wrote to on the rites of eating, in which was visible an act of reverence, and gratitude 'for what Nature's bounty and grace of spirit can create', back to the offering of mammoth-marrow before the last glaciation.)

How tonic it was through all my days to find admired lines by Auden coming unasked for, and for no immediate reason, into my thinking and feeling –

> *In the deserts of the heart*
> *Let the healing fountain start,*
> *In the prison of his days*
> *Teach the free man how to praise.*

What tonic expectation it launched to pick up the letters from the floor and find that daddy-long-legs handwriting on an envelope from New York or Kirchstetten. Thinking of Auden aroused only one disappointment, though I half expected it. I was driving home from France and knew Auden was one of the two favoured candidates for the year's Nobel Prize, and that the winner's name would be on the one o'clock news bulletin of English radio. I knew that the other candidate, the other likely winner of the one prize that seemed worth the bestowal, was Beckett, on account, I suppose, in chief, of *Waiting for Godot*. So we drew in beside a lane in Normandy under some pine trees, turned on the transistor, and waited. And it was Beckett, and I damned the gentlemen of the Swedish Academy for a brutish impercipience, and a sentimental, not to say provincial choice.

The worst moment to come was when I pushed open a neighbour's door, on a late September evening in 1973 and she said 'You've heard the news – Auden is dead.' A cold wind blew in at that moment on the warmth that had been for me and for so many others as well, part of the weather of a lifetime.

In the weeks after Wystan died and when the jackals were beginning to fasten on him, I felt all the more how curiously and cynically, and ignorantly too, so many people had managed to speak of that famous line by Wystan

We must love one another or die

(in his poem 'September 1st, 1939') as a naivety and as if its truth were negated by the way we had taken again in Europe and the East to hating each other and killing each other and as if those sour commentators hadn't an inkling of the admonitions and pronouncements by St John which Auden was adopting, that we should love one another and that who 'loveth not his brother abideth in death'.

12 – LOUIS MACNEICE

Time on horseback under a Roman arch.

Even a still life is alive
And in your Chardin the appalling unrest of the soul
Exudes from the dried fish and the brown jug and the bowl.

Quite a bit could be learnt about English writers at present and recently by discovering their reactions to Louis MacNeice since his death in 1963 – their reaction not *vis-à-vis* his poems directly, but in a reverse of reasonable generosity.

He is our Pasternak, less open to be sure, less concerned for us all, yet he is one of those poets who seem to excite the jealousy of contemporaries and slightly younger poets who were less gifted than he was. Here is a poet who propped up raffish bars near Broadcasting House, an elegant man and an elegant writer, and a scholar from an Oxford college and an English public school and English prep school, who looked all the same like the habitué of a zinc-topped bar among an Irish company painted by Jack Yeats, who yet was open to what Russia's Pasternak frequently spoke of in such terms as loyalty to the Earth of the World, a poet nourishing and nourished by an image of life 'compounded by all the testimonies of our senses and all the aspects of our conciousness' – 'all the juices of the earth, gradually spread by the flow of time,' to quote from Pasternak's *Letters to Georgian Friends*.

Talk of that specific kind often, I would say too often, embarrasses English poets (and novelists, and readers), leaving them at the same time jealous, and always wanting to go on in a restless way to something different, something new.

In the days when I knew Louis MacNeice (if I ever did; and could anyone ever have known him?) there were few translations around of Pasternak's prose or verse. Louis never had occasion to speak of Pasternak *vis-à-vis* the Earth, even supposing that he could or would

have done so. The same would have applied to translations from the
Japanese, nature images from the Japanese, *haiku* which the English
find embarrassing, partly because they serve by themselves as
poems, such very brief poems, with implications, yes, but not woven
into explanations at length.

Would Louis, who could speak of snow and roses against a
window, have enjoyed the *haiku* of the great Japanese masters?
Would Louis have enjoyed the bare lists that Sei Shōnagon inserted
a thousand years ago in her *Pillow Book*, had a translation been
available to him?

> *Duck eggs*
> *An urn containing the relics of some holy person*
> *Wild pinks*
>
> *The voice of someone who blows his nose*
> *while he is speaking.*
>
> *The expression of a woman plucking her eyebrows*

Extra lucky is the poet, in our tradition, like Wordsworth, when
someone spots for him, sifts and selects for him, proffers him a
foxglove, or hail making the dry dead holly leaves jump and dance.

Whether Louis had only himself to rely on, or whether, though I
doubt it, he ever had some Dorothy Wordsworth of his own, I don't
know; but there is no doubting the degree of his delights, or the way
so many poets have envied and turned against him on that score.

If he was reticent, his reticence was of a strange order and was
inconsistent. He could be embarassingly silent. A conversation came
to a halt. Who was going to break the silence and bridge the silent
interruption? His lack of usual reticence, too, could be sudden,
startling and improbable, rather like his appearance, dark, handsome, tall, well-dressed; then, looked at more closely, almost
squalid. There were friends of his I did not care for, also dark,
handsome, tall, though not squalid – aloof friends in the Foreign
Office and the like, who had been at school with him at Marlborough, cycling on the Wiltshire downs in white shorts when the

Queen Anne's Lace was in full bloom, almost hiding every track. Were they given to conversation? The chief of them at Marlborough and later at Oxford, now regarded as a non-person, was Anthony Blunt, and to be sure the two of them did not talk all the time about politics or communism, Louis having been the least political, the least either secret or open revolutionary among the Oxford poets of his time. If Louis looked so elegant at first glance, a second glance revealed that he had, as a rule, the dirtiest of finger nails. He had a dog, a tall elegant Borzoi. Just the dog for him, it seemed, who bent slowly and gracefully around the corners of tables and chairs, but goodness, how dirty that Betsy was underneath, what brown matted curls she had, and how she stank! Louis (as well as an idiot brother) had a sister, Elizabeth, pale as he was dark, and even more remote, who would come round and fetch his shock-headed child Dan from nursery teas and afternoons in Keats Grove. When the incomplete autobiography he wrote was published after his death, this Lady Nicholson added notes denying one or other incident and admission of his unhappiness in their childhood home, which was in the rectory at Carrickfergus. The stories Louis told me made his father, the very Anglican yet very Irish parson, later on a Bishop, seem as remote as himself and his sister. I believed – and believe – his stories of Medusa heads perched at the end of his nursery cot, of coloured cats which appeared to him terrifyingly as eidetic images, of silence enforced by the threats (and punishments) with which his nanny kept him in order and kept him from screaming out to his widowed father and his guests in the dining-room or drawing-room downstairs. To these Irish beginnings prep school days in Dorset under one of the Powys brothers and the summer vision of streams white with water crowfoot came as something of an antidote. He told me of much more in this line than he admits in that autobiography, and at that time, when he took over my garden flat in Keats Grove (which I could no longer afford after the collapse of the *Morning Post*) he once astounded me by saying, or alleging or imagining, that he liked nothing better than discussing the intimacies and privacies of life with his friends, the intimacies of their lives or his own life. I would sooner have attempted to interest the Holy Ghost or the Lord Chancellor in my private affairs, yet in a way I did feel intimate with Louis. I never set foot with him on a patch of grass, never shared a view with him which wasn't urban, yet I saw him always in terms of his delight in the Earth of the World.

Mild and peaceful he was, or seemed, as a rule, or wanted to be:

> *Let all these so ephemeral things*
> *Be somehow permanent like the swallow's tangent wings:*
> *Goodbye to you, this day remember is Christmas, this morn*
> *They say, interpret it in your own way, Christ is born.*

Romantic he was, if sceptical. The purple-skirted fuchsia flowers of the Gaeltacht swung in his mind, he fancied for a while, so he remarked to me once, being a seal secure and at ease in the green swell among the Connemara rocks.

Fierce he could be, distinctly, in words, in occasional controversy when his values were assailed, as the Ulsterman St John Ervine, who fancied himself as a superior and scornful controversialist, once learnt when battered by Louis in an exchange of letters in the *Observer*.

Rather it is as if my Louis MacNeice ended with the dark character I thought I knew in the Thirties, ended with the famous (or have I to say the once famous?) 'Bagpipe Music':

> *It's no good the merrygoround, it's no go the rickshaw,*
> *All we want is a limousine and a ticket for the peepshow,*
> *Their knickers are made of crepe-de-chine, their*
> *   shoes are made of python,*
> *Their halls are lined with tiger rugs and their walls*
> *   with heads of bison*

which I published, I am glad to say, in January 1938, after it had been turned down by the *Listener* as perhaps in those days – but why exactly? – too much for the Powers or the Governors or the Director-General of the British Broadcasting Corporation.

I do not pretend to have known Louis well. I even felt, I won't say

75

afraid of him, but a little embarrassed by him, a little relieved when the door closed behind him.

But I still wonder if any one who knew Louis, anyone of all those who formed his company of friends at school and university, as an undergraduate and later in Birmingham and London Universities as a teacher of the classics, and in the BBC, knew him in any depth?

If you doubt my remark that Louis MacNeice is our Pasternak and should be reverenced as such, and you haven't penetrated that deep into the large corpus of his *Collected Poems*, read and re-read 'Thalassa', which seems to have been one of the last poems he wrote:

> *Run out the boat, my broken comrades;*
> *Let the old seaweed crack, the surge*
> *Burgeon oblivious of the last*
> *Embarkation of feckless men,*
> *Let every adverse force converge –*
> *Here we must needs embark again.*
>
> *Run up the sail, my heartsick comrades;*
> *Let each horizon tilt and lurch –*
> *You know the worst: your wills are fickle,*
> *Your values blurred, your hearts impure*
> *And your past life a ruined church –*
> *But let your poison be your cure.*
>
> *Put out to sea, ignoble comrades,*
> *Whose record shall be noble yet;*
> *Butting through scarps of moving marble*
> *The narwhal dares us to be free;*
> *By a high star our course is set,*
> *Our end is Life. Put out to sea.*

– and then ask how many nobler poems you know from recent years – or recent decades. I must admit that poem came to me as rather a surprise, admire Louis MacNeice and respect him as I did.

13 – STEPHEN SPENDER

*The failure of cathedrals and the declared
insanity of our rulers.*

Stephen Spender told a story of how he proposed to a friend that they should take a brief holiday out of London. 'Choose where you would like to go,' said Stephen, having in his own mind a few days at somewhere, some such extension of London as Brighton or Eastbourne or Folkestone. 'Well,' said his friend. 'What about Rome? I've never seen Rome.'

Stephen hadn't much money, but the holiday was his idea, so to Rome they went, which was where I ran into them one afternoon on the Spanish Steps. Perhaps we all felt out on a limb and in need of a little English talk and London gossip, so we talked and talked in the English tea-rooms.

We talked and talked several times more in the next few days, but I don't recall that we spent much time or thought on the grandeurs of Rome or even mentioned Keats dying in tubercular agony on the Spanish Steps. We were in the Rome of Fascism and Mussolini, and I did go with Stephen – otherwise my recollection is nearly a blank – to a vast exhibition listing the Fascist Martyrs and commemorating that March on Rome which Mussolini – there were the enlarged photos to prove it – led in spats. Soft, sad, noble, potted music played round the glass cases shrining clubs and shillelaghs which had been carried by the faithful dead.

It was the shillelaghs which pulled the trigger for Stephen. At the sight of them this long poet let out a sudden enormous echoing laugh, ridicule of the nastily ridiculous. Attendants with more shillelaghs might suddenly have darted out of invisible openings and laid about us, and thrown us out on the pavement. But no, no one noticed.

I went off to Sardinia, only to be driven back sooner than I had expected by too much of myself alone, solaced just a little in the Gennargentu Mountains by a first whiff of the unbelievable sharp scent of wild cyclamen and a sight of lean ridgy swine – swine not pigs – which had just trotted out of Dürer's engraving of the Prodigal Son. I rejoined Stephen, still rather afraid of him, up the coast from Rome, learning more of him than I had guessed before, and feeling rather less of what I had imagined to be his disapproval. It was there we saw the twinkling of fireflies, each of us, for the first time. Then back I went to London carrying with me, for Faber and Faber in Russell Square, the typescript of the novel Stephen had been working on every day.

Thin and tall as a light-tower at some harbour entrance, Stephen belonged to towns, capital towns, throwing around a light of his own, already felt as something special and already mocked by the irresponsive and irreverent. Auden, you could already feel from all he had published so far, and despite all the shortsightedness of which he complained, belonged to everywhere, factory squalor of Birmingham, and the Long Mynd:

> *Who stands, the crux left of the watershed,*
> *On the wet road between the chafing grass*
> *Below him sees dismantled washing-floors,*
> *Snatches of tramline, running to a wood.*

MacNeice felt downland and wild roses. Stephen's climate wasn't even London: it was the highest heaven of celestial fire, the Empyrean of man, art, poetry, and politics or social possibility and perfection; and just that, coupled with a naive intensity, made him hard to live up to: he really did think of the 'truly great', as in the poem on which his gathering fame and name depended, 'continually', though I daresay it would have been better to think of them intermittently. 'Continually' – thinking of the not merely great but the truly great, continually – invited a Max Beerbohm drawing.

For someone with such genuine holy thoughts Stephen could too easily be misinterpreted. Why did this tall holy youth cultivate acquaintanceships – which he had begun to do already when he was an undergraduate – with so many poets and other writers whom others of us despised? Because he was feathering his own literary career ahead of time? So many of us said, and it was unfair. He wanted to know about poets. And hadn't this tall exotic holy youth a pretty sharp tongue of his own? He had; but wasn't it directed as often as not against acts or behaviour which contradicted or insulted the literary Empyrean?

I turned up *Spender, Stephen, b*, 1909, in a recent *Who's Who* to have a clearer understanding of all he had been up to publicly through middle into old age, and was amazed at all I found, the lectureships, the professorships, Poet in Residence in the Library of Congress, and more yet. And then my mind went back to Stephen saying long ago how he, Stephen Spender, would like, were it only possible or conceivable, to be a Goethe for our century, our Western world, instructing us like Goethe from Weimar. He will forgive me if I add, on his own authority, that he had or felt that he had more than a little to live down from his Hampstead childhood and adolescence, if I mention that his father, an Oxford double first, who made the right marriage, and climbed mountains, and filled the right political, cultured, Liberal niche, was also a journalist, a political, professional, Liberal journalist none too well thought of in Fleet Street, where I used to hear him referred to as 'Lloyd George's Jackal', in whose hearing nothing confidential should be let slip or it 'would be round the ghetto in an hour'.

He embarrassed his two sons by ostentatiously kissing them goodbye – how his beard tickled – on their doorstep in Frognal just when the other boys were likely to be passing on their morning way to University College School.

In the celebrated triarchy and hierarchy of the Thirties Stephen stood for lyricism without soppiness and for the dutiful behaviour of the artist. If one's perception of that duty in its finer degrees fell short, if one felt guilty on that score, Stephen's disapproval, real or imagined, did not make for self-confidence.

Sharp-tongued Stephen believed that I had been the first to call him 'the Rupert Brooke of the Depression'. I wouldn't have dared. Funny, understandable (though physically awkward Stephen was never as handsome as Brooke), that unfair description was invented by Norman Cameron.

14 – DYLAN THOMAS

What was worse, if, as often happened, we caught him out
Stealing or pinching the maid's backside, he would leer,
With a cigarette on his lip and a shiny snout,
With a hint: 'You and I are all in the same galère?'
Norman Cameron

Ditch, Dirty Dylan, the Changeling, the Ugly Suckling, the Disembodied Gland – these early private names were still not invented. The rumour which was to increase to the legend of the purest genius had scarcely begun, at this moment, in the Thirties, when, in a tea- room, an awkward *Mr* Thomas faced an awkward, also an unconvinced, *Mr* Myself across a corner table. The tea-room was in a courtyard between the dull quiet of the Temple and the dull mumble of Fleet Street.

Young *Mr* Thomas was up from Cwmdonkin Drive, Swansea, in big London, where poets existed. He was uncertain of his part. He might, sitting there in the corner below the grey panes, have been acting a new Rimbaud. In features, still unpoached at this time, he looked rather like the Rimbaud portrayed in a group by Fantin Latour. But he had not heard of Rimbaud, in Swansea; he wore a different poetic uniform, imitated, I rather think, from a frontispiece of the young Rossetti. Curls thatched his head, a Bohemian poetry tie flowed down and out below his soft collar. He talked poetry, his biographers might be surprised to learn. Young but not quite so young *Mr* Myself suspiciously regarded this tie, and suspiciously heard a proffer of names he had not expected. Rossetti was one of them, Francis Thompson was another, James Thomson (BV) was a third. Stephen Spender, though, was a fourth.

Names, as I say, were proffered: were held out, withdrawn, held out again, much as one might offer bits of food to a beast of uncertain nature and temper with whom one found oneself unexpectedly but ineluctably roomed or cabined or boxed.

81

Our presence with each other was Stephen Spender's indirect doing. Odd poems above the name Dylan Thomas had appeared in the *Sunday Referee*, in the Poet's Corner conducted by the odd Victor Neuberg, a little man who for a while had been changed and enlarged into a camel by Aleister Crowley (a story invented, perhaps, by Thomas). I think Stephen Spender must have been one of the first unloony persons to comment on these poems and to enquire about their author, so fixing a label to him as 'someone to be watched'. I recall Spender assuring me at any rate that I ought to ask Dylan Thomas for contributions to *New Verse*. He may have given me Dylan's address. Letters had gone to Wales, letters and poems in pale blue ink in that slow, leftward-sloping, pre-adolescent, unpersuasive hand from which Dylan never freed himself, had returned from 5 Cwmdonkin Drive and perhaps another Swansea address; and at this encounter we now *mistered* each other and investigated each other and *mistered* each other again in the law-clerks' grey tea-room.

Dylan had not yet succeeded enough, or sloughed off enough of lowest-middle-class Swansea, to resemble the painting of him by Augustus John. He was not so cocky. He needed assurance, with which he was never generously and liberatingly supplied. But London quickly intimidated him less, and was entered by him more frequently. Art-adulating zanies in Parton Street, near Red Lion Square, frequenting that café on one side and that bookshop on the other, first eyed him like schoolboy butterfly collectors eyeing a supposed Camberwell Beauty on the wing. They were persons of a kind needing shots of the notion of art as others need shots of insulin, of a kind put on heat by the slightest contact with artists of any nature. If Mr John Malcolm Brinnin's America proved fantastically full of such people, whom Dylan learnt rapidly to use and kept on using till they lapped around his death in a New York hospital, the London supply of them is never to be despised. Praise from them makes one sceptical, nearly always in my experience with reason, especially if the chorus of praise begins with them.

Modernism's higher command, whether it might be Wyndham Lewis hidden in Notting Hill Gate or T. S. Eliot cocooned in his publishing office in Russell Square, was not impressed; Eliot at least was offered and considered – and then refused – a collection of his poems. Nor, although Stephen Spender helped to float him, at least by talk, was Dylan Thomas then sure enough of himself to approach the Inner Command of the Thirties – I use this image of a 'command', in either case, approximately, or as a metaphor. If the zanies of all levels bored him, at first, if others repelled him or scared him, Dylan found friends in London who were independent of the Commands. One was Norman Cameron, now dead, who was linked to Robert Graves rather than to Eliot. Another was Bernard Spencer, linked only to himself. I was a third, Ruthven Todd, the universal friend newly down from Edinburgh, became a fourth.

We caused him less trepidation, kept him less on edge. Our appetites, our laziness or easygoingness, our scepticism, were less forbidding. He could enjoy with us verbal jokes and myths and inventions which committed him to no decision, no ideal of mental or spiritual conduct. He could trust himself to clown, to swear, to talk of women, or sex; he could borrow our beds, our underclothes and our cash, be washed, on occasion be mended and dry-cleaned by our wives whom he could attempt to lay sooner or later; and he could learn from us co-ordinating signs and landmarks of a Thirties London.

If I was Doc, Doc Terry, or Terry, to him, Norman Cameron, that aloof and blunt and uncommonsensible poet, was rapidly christened Normal by Dylan Thomas – much as a large man in the RAF is christened Tiny.

Serial jokes and myths – word jokes and word myths – ran through our association as they run in families; especially a serial myth of advertisements for *night custard*, a Thomas invention and patent, an alchemical liquid almost, which satisfied, with every obscene twist, that 'night starvation' already postulated, with Cameron's help, in the advertisements of a beverage. We could make fun-figures out of critics, prigs, editors, poets, holy lady poets from Cambridge, whom we did not like; we could give them names and play with them.

Also we could advance our curious elf in the way of reputation, and in the way at least of making drink money, if not a living. In one character I could publish poems by him in *New Verse*, in another I could give him books to review on the *Morning Post*.

Which books? Thrillers; of these week by week he devoured half-a-dozen or more, reviewed them or, as the writers would have thought, misreviewed them, with a gay improbable wordage, and then sold them. Between ourselves, and the zanies, and Swansea, Dylan Thomas now appeared, disappeared, appeared again – usually without money.

Rossetti and the waterfall tie soon vanished. Dylan Thomas found that London preferred to aesthetic debauch, or its uniform, the Toughish Boy, the Boy with a Load of Beer, in and out, so boringly, of the pubs. The part was more congenial and more genuine, with a scope for virtuosity. It was defensive, already – defence, release, escape – though this was not yet the habit of the whole.

Here, then, for us, certainly for me, was Ditch, here was Dirty Dylan – since we retaliated with our own names. Generally he was the Toughish Boy elsewhere, he reappeared from zanies, from sluts (often combined), from drunkenness, he needed washing, so did his shirts, he needed a little regularity, a little sobriety; and accepted them all, for short whiles. In fears of disease he had to be taken to doctors. I found him one day in the bath in my flat in Keats Grove, pitying himself and mocking himself in verbal antics because a pink rash beautifully enflamed him back and front. Hauled down by bus to the neighbourhood of the British Museum, to an Irish doctor, Dylan stripped to his meagre body. The doctor assured him he had no need to worry, after all, laughed at him, and pulled down a coloured chart, still more lividly pink than Dylan himself, to give an accurate warning of what the symptoms might be another time. For a minor illness he did retire before long to Wales and to its more comfortable familiar things, begging me by letter that retreat and illness should not be mentioned in London for fear of curtailing his activities when he recovered and returned.

I agree to Dylan's companionableness, to his clowning, fooling, mocking talent, to, best of all, a certain primal quality, rooted far behind our backs in suburban Swansea, in chock-a-block Welsh cemeteries in the hilly viridian farms between Laugharne and Llanstephan or in the Gower; but he was also the snotty troll, *to himself enough*, when it suited him, he had also grown from the changeling lifted from under the foxgloves and set in the proper and decent calvinist Welsh bed. He was cartilaginous, out of humanity, the Disembodied Gland, which was my coinage, Ditch, which was Norman Cameron's, the Ugly Suckling, which was Bernard Spencer's, indicating a wilful and at times nasty babyishness. When he disappeared, it was a relief; when he reappeared, a pleasure.

Adaptation or adjustment continued. One heard less from Dylan about James Thomson (B V), who had satisfied in him both a morbidity and a leaning to grandiloquence, less about Francis Thompson (for whose effect on Dylan Thomas the inquisitive should turn to the *Ode to the Setting Sun*, in which stuffy insufferable poem they will find the pattern of Dylan Thomas lines, questions, verbs and other tricks –

> *It is the falling star that trails the night –*
>
> *Who scarfed her with the morning –*
>
> *Who lit the furnace of the mammoth's heart?*
> *Who shagged him like Pilatus ribbed flanks? –*
>
> *Who girt dissolved lightnings in the grape?*
> *Summered the opal with an Irised flush?*

– as well as the *fons et origo* of the Thomas attitude of birth-copulation-death:

> *For birth hath in itself the germ of death,*
> *But death hath in itself the germ of birth.*
> *It is the falling acorn buds the tree,*
> *The falling rain that bears the greenery,*
> *The fern-plants moulder when the ferns arise,*
> *For there is nothing lives but something dies,*
> *And there is nothing dies but something lives.*

It would be exaggeration to say that he substituted much other reading. He seldom opened books in these days, unless they were thrillers or dreadfuls. Having introduced himself as a poet, he ceased to talk of at any rate dead poets. He was innocent of learning or intellectualism or intellectual appetite, so much, so obviously, that one now felt sure a development, even a continuance, would be impossible beyond a point which must quite soon be reached. Dylan might seem a hole in the ground up through which life or a biological and mortal essence was sulphurously boiling, bubbling, troubling, confusing; but he was not worshipful (we should have worshipped him readily if he had been): he was adding nothing viable to the automatic acceptances and accumulations of childhood, which were not inexhaustible. He might only have more explication to do. It seemed to me also (it still does) that a keener sense in his appreciators and magnifiers would have recognized how much decayed romanticism there is in his phrases and rhythms, much of it twisted arsy-versily and new-applied, as if Sir William Watson, in *The Times*, had taken to a symbolism of up wanton up. Actually the line is Shelley-cum-Keats-Thomson-Thompson-Thomas – with no intervention at all of Hopkins, whatever was alleged posthumously. Afterwards he read verse with an allied over-ripeness appealing to the poesy-mindedness of American art-impresarios, BBC producers and all *les Belges* exactly as the energetic amalgam of the bosoms, thighs, blood, swords and beards of a coloured Troy appeals and seems magnificent across the wide screen of the cinema. I published poems by Dylan doubting (as I still do) whether they had not a softer inside below a soft outside and whether they were not technically and formally as puerile as a film panorama – preferring poems harder and better rooted by his Swansea friend Glyn Jones, which actually were related to the glittering severities of Welsh poetry – to Dafydd ap Gwilym rather than Francis Thompson.

Dylan, though, was also something other than his poems, other than the oblong grubby scraps off a lined pad on which they appeared or from which they were amalgamated. He had enough magnetism, though one leg of the magnet might exert repulsion, to cause worry by his upsets or difficulties. We may not have detected every symptom or joined up the ones we did detect, we may not entirely have seen (it was clearer afterwards) how Dylan was being compelled to live beyond his spiritual or intellectual income – or capital; a compulsion which explained some of his defensive clowning and a good deal of his load of beer. Occasionally, though, he hinted at TB, and spitting blood; he was too frequently ill or out of sorts. It was after some such hints, after drinking too much had sobered him and frightened him a little, after the beginning of the genius-hunting parties, that Dylan and I went off for some weeks, in a summer before the war, to Donegal.

There was a valley above the Atlantic entered by no road, not even by a well-defined path, over a ridge of rock, peat and heather. In this valley of Glen Lough between Ardara and Killybegs, I knew a solitary farmer and his wife. A year or two before, the place had been discovered by the American artist Rockwell Kent, who liked its wilderness and loneliness between mountains, or mountains and lakes, and the sea. He had concreted a donkey-shed into a sleeping-room and studio, and had abandoned it. It was in that room, on the edge of a small stream from the lakes, that Dylan and I lived for a while, building turf fires to dry ourselves out and keeping a quart bottle of potheen – illegal, colourless whiskey – hidden in a potato patch outside, below a lushness of chickweed. If indeed he had been in danger of TB, I daresay he ought not to have been in the dampness and softness of Ireland; but here he was drinking less potheen, at any rate, than he had drunk of beer and spirits in London, and less porter than milk and buttermilk.

The Swansea Changeling, who might at any time go back to his people, waded through mixed flames of loosestrife and corn marigold which floored the valley. From the cliffs he watched gannets dropping and flecking the Atlantic; or climbing steeply to the lakes at the back of the farm and the converted stable, we shouted up to the surrounding mountains *We are the Dead*, for the multiple echo to reply in sequence *We are the Dead, the Dead, the Dead*. We shouted so at the mountains above the lake one evening till we frightened ourselves, stumbling down afterwards through heather

87

and fern and sog to the comfort of the cottage, where Dylan
stretched stained white feet, Swansea feet, to the warm turf,
alongside the brown, huge feet of the farmer Dan Ward. At times we
sneaked down the enormous cliffs to a cold soul-tightening ocean
and sang the 'Ram of Derbyshire' to black seals. There was no sand,
no gravel, below those cliffs, only white pebbles shaped like eggs or
heads by Brancusi. We drew faces on them with black crayon, we
named them, set them against rock, and cracked them, with fling
after fling of other huge white pebbles, into literary nothingness –
since the names were of authors – and literary oblivion. Several faces
were those of people who were to find Dylan, to Dylan's dangerous
surprise, a vessel of later holiness.

I do not know how much, if at all, Dylan was moved by this
peculiar valley in which man was camping as he camps so small in the
cruel wilderness paintings and etchings by Hercules Seghers. It is
again, though, my feeling that he received only what was given to him
by childhood's environment of place, person, and literature.

> *Stroke and a stress that stars and storms deliver,*
> *That guilt is hushed by, hearts are flushed by and melt –*

In a way he knew that energizing, quietening, flushing and melting
influence, that preamble to a deeper poetry; but, in Hopkins's added
words, what did Dylan Thomas *fable*, what central reality did he then
miss, what reality *riding time like a river*?

After about a fortnight I had to go home, Dylan staying in the glen
for several more weeks, looked after by Dan Ward and Rose Ward,
who felt his magnetism – to their cost, because he left suddenly one
day, walking over the mountains towards Wales or London and Soho
pubs without paying them (though he had ample money) a penny of
the agreed sum for all his food and his lodging.

Certainly out of memory I could dredge other details, it might be
meetings of Dylan Thomas and George Orwell, in a Hampstead
bookshop in which Orwell worked, then less known than Dylan
himself, it might be the nature of drawings in coloured chalks, inept,
powdery, lurid, like horror-film images, or horror-comic images,

green and pink essays of an amateur expressionism, which Dylan left with me and which were destroyed in the war. 'Only from the work the biography acquires significance' – so it has been declared by one of the heralds of a great committed poet of mankind (and I happen to be writing this in his town, which is Tübingen, above his reflective river). 'No life' – no detail of life – 'concerns us that had not found adequate expression and shape'. Ask then whether the work, in this case, – but the answer must be your affair – contradicts the life. Or was there with Dylan Thomas too atrocious a war between what was given and what so temptingly was dangled and accepted?

15 – NORMAN CAMERON

Shepherdess, show me now where I may sleep

Norman Cameron was another Scot, from Edinburgh, but I hardly realized the fact. Did I ever hear him mention Scotland? It was himself he insisted on, not a Scotch self; a human self. I knew vaguely he had been at school at Fettes, which was no more than a name to me. Otherwise he seemed as much a Southern Englishman, as much a user of the English language as any of us. Partition or a cultural sub-nationalism would have seemed to him pointless, even ridiculous. His English, the English he spoke, the English he wrote, had no trace of Scotch accent or Scotch peculiarity. A patriotic Scot mightn't care for this human neutrality, might put it down to a migration from Fettes (which was also Ruthven Todd's school) to Oxford. Did he look like a Lowland or Edinburgh Scot? No more than the next man who was tall and thin and blonde. I never thought of this most honest and open of friends as other than the self I loved, until Ruthven Todd, after Norman's death, wrote me one of his interminable letters, a letter which went on and on like his talk, page after page, telling me what he knew of Norman's origins and early keepings, or what he had discovered by that biographical ferreting into the living or the dead, the recently dead or the long dead, at which he was so good.

I had supposed – perhaps some aspects, almost judicial, always rational, outspeaking aspects of Norman's character seemed to fit – that Norman's father had been a judge. But no. This poet who saw things so plainly, this original maker of myth, symbol and metaphor, this writer who seemed, but only seemed, one realized, on a wiser inspection, to exist in the stylistic and propositioned pocket of his greatest friend, Robert Graves, was the son of a distinguished Edinburgh cleric, who was Senior Presidency Chaplain at Bombay, and he was born in Coorg, the smallest of the Indian provinces. His father died, and his mother his brothers and a sister, came home to Edinburgh. From Fettes he went to Oriel College, Oxford. At Oxford he knew Auden, and before their Oxford days he and Auden had each contributed to the 1923–4 volume of *Public School Verse* (in which Auden's name was misprinted 'W. H. Arden'). At Oxford, though I knew of him, I did not know this undergraduate, who was to serve – for a while – with the Colonial Educational Service in Nigeria (for that African phase of his life, see Norman on himself quoted by Robert Graves in his introduction, after his death, to Norman's *Collected Poems*). In London I think I owed my introduction to Norman to that rather mysterious Gilbert Armitage who led me first to Wyndham Lewis and tried to make me publish poems scribbled on crumpled lengths of paper by John Betjeman. Gilbert knew everyone, and everything.

Once you gained Norman's good opinion of yourself, you could be pardoned for most things – if not for what he considered literary misdemeanours, or some literary misdemeanours. Others could be overlooked if they did not invite too serious a conflict of loyalties. On one occasion, when I was in hospital recovering from a minor operation and feeling free of responsibilities, I wrote an indiscrete letter to Robert Graves about some of the literary company I knew him to have kept. Graves was incensed, he thought the letter an impertinence, which it was, I suppose, and he proposed to pay me out by writing and complaining to my employer, the *Morning Post*. I was scared. My wife was ill and had started the long and expensive process of dying. The last thing I could afford was a total loss of a well-paid job. Who came to the rescue, and not entirely on humanitarian grounds? Norman Cameron, of course. However much I had offended Robert Graves, I had so to say a sufficiency of personal capital with Norman, who intervened and made Robert hold his hand, much as he disapproved of that letter.

At Oxford he had known Stephen Spender and then and there after, now we were all in London, he did not approve of what he thought were Stephen's activities in courting the Literary Establishment, the old guard of letters whose goings on we despised.

Norman's description of Stephen Spender as 'the Rupert Brooke of the Depression' stuck, and went the rounds, and must have seemed particularly unfair to those who had also known Rupert Brooke, than whom no one then was more of a poetic Aunt Sally for the young. Asked about Rupert Brooke, kind well-balanced E. M. Forster – if I may raid the first volume of his *Selected Letters* – spoke of Rupert Brooke's beauty and charm and serenity, disliked the way he was going 'down to posterity as a sort of St Sebastian, haloed by the Dean of St Paul's, and hymned by the *Morning Post* as the Evangelist of anti-Germanism'. He found him hard – 'and I don't envy anyone who applied to him for sympathy' – a character which wouldn't fit Stephen Spender.

Norman was someone who turned up. One wore a hat in those pre-war days – or Norman did. I would come back to Hampstead, to Wildwood Terrace behind the *Bull and Bush*, open the door and find a hat on the wall, over a suitcase. I would go into the sitting-room and find the chessmen laid out, and behind the chessmen Norman Cameron asleep and snoring slightly, under his crown of hair (how did that hat fit on the crown?).

He had come to stay, without announcement. One might as well have found him asleep on – or in – the spare bed. But he wanted a game of chess as well as a sleep.

I realize the traffic was always this way. Norman came, Norman, as I say, turned up. I don't remember seeing where he lived, at this time, either while his Hamburg wife Elfrieda was alive (she was to lie before long under a stone carved by Henry Moore), or later when he was for a while alone and complaining of his need 'of silk stockings among his socks'. Did I know of him in the Balearic Islands with Robert Graves – or at his work for an advertising agency? No. Norman was his presence or his poems. If he possessed a home, it was almost as if he carried it folded in his pocket, or in the suitcase which lay under his improbable hat, or as if his character warmed him in the cold, or kept off the rain, and included no room for average concerns or possessions, for books (but he knew about poems), for scholarship (though he had read Greats at Oriel), for the 'literary life'. No home; also, I repeat, no country. How odd it was to see him inserted with national aplomb, in a book of Scotch Verse. Writing in English, neither Englishman nor Scotsman, but only man, he would have thought – a point I emphasize again –sectionalism of the kind infantile, as it is, and beside the point.

What marked him was the certainty and rightness of being right, without priggery or conciousness of the matter. When Dylan Thomas, often the victim of Norman's incorruptibility, used to call him 'Normal', this meant different things. It could have meant, for instance, that story of Elfrieda's, of what happened on their wedding night, which amused her so much, when she and Norman performed and Norman said in his half-muffled tone 'Thanks very much', and turned over and slept. Also it meant that Norman always knew what should be the essence, for example, of right literary (and other) behaviour, of wrong literary (and other) behaviour, or wrong literary (and other) shamefulness, which made him frightening a little, if at the same time more to be loved, more always to be admired, one's guardian against one's own sham or evasions (no wonder he translated Villon and Rimbaud).

As man, he was contemptuous, in his slightly lofty (lofty rather than high) and husky voice, about most kinds of ambition, particularly the arse-licking and the search for position which some authors and artists indulge in. But malicious he was not, and his contempt ('the Rupert Brooke of the Depression', and so on) was liable to change to laughter – 'laughter supervened':

> *Laughter, the sunlight in the cucumber,*
> *The innermost resource that does not fail.*

You may remember that in the poem from which those two lines came, he was laughing at the dead – he had come back, 'Marco Polo, traveller', from the ridiculous kingdom of the dead – 'with what a tale' of their repetition of the political and military trivialities of living.

A vision of this constant Marco Polo recurs to me, Norman – very long and slight, white-faced, shock-headed, someone who had strayed for a little out of London – at work on a hillside in Wiltshire. Some weeks before, my wife pregnant and unable to come with us, Norman and I had walked across North Wiltshire and discovered down below an escarpment an empty cottage under the blackness of a yew. I bought this cottage and the two of us now went there for several weekends, moving lumps of chalk, digging out nuttal stumps, cleaning away earth. Hard labour wasn't Norman's *métier* and he wore mittens, and he kept his overcoat on; and again, as if this cottage business was a sample of the triviality or the oddness of living, in which he was an unexpected and surprised Marco Polo, 'laughter supervened'. He pushed, he tugged, he invented phrases, he fell, he slid on frosty grass, and laughed. Had the hill behind the cottage opened, had Norman disappeared inside it, into his own land, laughing, but fed up with his spare manufacture of myths for our situation, on the superficial earth, I should have been only a little surprised. In a human way he was almost inhuman.

It may be that he did disappear in that manner, in the end. We were separated by the war, so that I knew the rest of him only by hearsay, his drinking, his dying; but I cannot conceive of a Cameron middle-aged or old. When he was young, when he was very alive, he moved at once towards the genuine in the writing or the art of his day, in its highest quality; he wrote or coined in good metal poems it would be ridiculous to attack (or to reject, I think). Like a Ransom, or a Rochester, or a George Herbert, he contrived his poems with an *ad hoc* scrupulosity of diction, allowing no trailing on, or trailing out, into superfluities. I cannot suppose that as a poet he would have changed very much, or widened, or become in any way a writer by habit. He could only have stopped, sooner or later, particularly if he had begun to recognize any treason in the words he put down, anything simply unnecessary, undictated, or commonplace. He was a literate original, not a literary man. Perhaps he should be thought of in the terms of that prose poem of Baudelaire's about the necessity of being drunk always, against the weight of time. But – 'what with? Wine, poetry or being good, please yourself, but get drunk.'

To get Norman right I should append Baudelaire's catalogue:

'And if now and then, on the steps of a palace, on the green grass of a ditch, in the glum loneliness of your room, you come to, your drunken condition abated or dissolved, ask the wind, ask the wave, the star, the bird, the clock, all that runs away, all that groans, all that wheels, all that sings, all that speaks, what time it is, and the wind, the wave, the star, the bird, the clock, will tell you *it is time to get drunk*! . . . with wine, with poetry or with being good. As you please.'

Norman tried all three, especially the second and the third. But that isn't right after all, because with him it was not a question of 'trying,' his state was his nature. Also I should remember to emphasize how much he mixed forgiveness and charity with his scorn: he could wither you, then protect you from yourself with a short smile, about the eyes and the mouth, of extraordinary attractiveness, himself always under the same regime of examination. He was tender, and not devious –

Shepherdess, show me now where I can sleep.

He did, all the same, find it none too easy to forgive Dylan Thomas, whose company had once afforded him – and myself too – such pleasure. That poem of his, 'The Dirty Little Accuser,' is about Dylan –

That insolent little ruffian, that crapulous lout.
When he quitted a sofa, he left behind him a smear.
My wife says he even tried to paw her about.

– and with reason. Read the account of Dylan, not a word of it, I am ready to believe, exaggerated or untrue, which A. J. P. Taylor, the historian, gives in his autobiography.

I shall add just one other thing, that if Norman was ever shocked, not at all in a Scotch puritan way, it was when a girl of his cheerfully spoke of some of her recent activities with schoolboys, with sixth form boys much younger than herself. Norman brought this beauty (she was a ballet dancer) to tea one afternoon in Keats Grove, and after she had gone off to Paddington in a cab and I was saying how delightful she was, how beautiful, how lithe, how unusual, etc., etc., he interjected 'Do you know what she told me yesterday when we were in bed? She told me nothing gave her such pleasure as the look in a schoolboy's eyes when she opened his flybuttons and manipulated him in a train, and he came over her hand.'

I think she told Norman that the last time she had pleasured a boy like that, it was in an empty carriage in the Cornish Riviera. Norman remarked on the scent she usually wore.

Perhaps after all Norman wasn't shocked by that admission or confession, only surprised, as most of us would be surprised, even now in 1984.

16 – HENRY MOORE

Henry Moore and I sat at dinner in the best hotel in Amsterdam, at the expense of the British Council, the war not so long over, and sent up requests to the orchestra, one of them, Henry's, not mine, for Charlie Chaplin's *Limelight* melody. (Henry was having one of those overseas exhibitions which were establishing his fame, I was lecturing – was it on Henry, or was it on Turner?).

Henry Moore and I and the British Council rep., Roger Hinks, who had been blamed for a scrubbing or at any rate too severe a cleaning of the Elgin Marbles, and had lost his British Museum job in consequence, ate roast goose on Sunday on the way to see the Van Gogh pictures in the Kröller-Müller Museum, among the sand dunes, playing *en route* the game of picking the celebrated artist of the past centuries we could most do without. We agreed on Hals. Henry spoke of the greatness, the scale of Turner, and reproved me, rather, for too much of an admiration for Klee, a miniaturist.

Henry Moore and I sat in a crowded Dutch tea-room enjoying the sound and the action of xylophone or zither music, and glad that the British Council had just agreed to pay substantial compensation to widows if anything slew artists or lecturers they sent abroad. 'We can have happy thoughts when we're bubbling down to the bottom,' said H.M.

H.M. and I went to the Rijksmuseum, Henry allowing me to look at no more than about one picture on the way to the 'Night Watch' and the surviving fragment of the 'Anatomy Lesson'. H.M. made for him a remark that was slightly acid – that 'If that man Bacon wanted to know what a hole in a human body looked like, he should come and look at the 'Anatomy Lesson'. I inveigled him into the print room to see – I was full of them at the time as images of man – the colour prints on cloth and the etchings on coloured paper by Hercules Seghers, Rembrandt's master.

H.M. and I were taken by the Director of the Stedelijk Museum down that Amsterdam street where the tarts exhibited themselves in lighted windows, enticing customers. One of them was knitting, a fat unprepossessing tart. 'She'll finish that jumper,' H.M. remarked, 'before she gets a customer.'

H.M. and I go to Rotterdam to an exhibition of drawings by Delacroix, and H.M. instructs me on shortcomings, after all, in Delacroix's draughtsmanship.

At home H.M. had furnished me with a coloured drawing for the jacket of my first book of poems, which I hope, on his account, is suitably expensive in its rarity. Nineteen-thirty-nine was the date of that book, *Several Observations*: and when the war was drawing to its close I sat up with H.M. in his Hertfordshire home renewing an old habit of endless cups of Yorkshire tea into the night, looking at drawings and photos – his own photos of his own work – while from time to time a fly-bomb boomed, luckily from a distance.

He was a good friend, a good consoler, a good adviser, in those long past years. He delicately pinched my young daughter's limbs, in the cradle, to feel the solidity of flesh; he advised me on the sensible conduct of a marriage, when to stick, when to give way. Like Wyndham Lewis, whom he used to admire when I first knew him (though Lewis was too sharp in the long run to fit with his gentleness), he was an educator, and in more than such matters as Rembrandt's paintings and Delacroix's drawings, and constructed form in Poussin's landscapes and sacred dances, and the quality of early paintings by the young John Piper whose company he told me to seek out.

Let me think a little more of him at random. He instructed me in the shapes of stones and bones, water-worn, wave-worn stones and bones. After the spectators thinned away from a private view of his work or a private view at the Leicester Galleries of the latest exhibition of the Seven and Five, that liveliest of art societies, we would go off through the dark to wonderful, cheap Soho dinners, myself happy in the company and little realizing the world fame that waited him.

Another recollection. Packs on our shoulders filled with saucepans and mugs and other household or kitchen impedimenta, we went down to Wiltshire and camped in that still empty cottage my American wife and I had just bought, Henry insisting that we make the most of that cottage since we would never enjoy fitting up another house so much as the first one that was our own; and round the overgrown garden, among the hazel clumps, he went, crouching for the best site for an outdoor loo, best for enjoying a huge view stretching away below the garden, and past the yew tree, like the landscape of Rubens's 'Château de Steen' in the National Gallery.

Perhaps that loo of plank and galvanized – it is still there, I think, though I long ago sold the cottage – should be preserved by the British Council or the National Trust. Admission 50*p*, a red cord across the seat.

Moore was sturdily at all times of his own mind – if 'sturdily' does not seem a patronizing adverb – long before his ultimate enthronement, his near deification, long before Picasso held up a luncheon party to finish looking through the first large album of his work, and then came in to his waiting guests, saying 'a grand artist'.

I suppose there is a touch of patronage – patronage of the sculptor who was a Yorkshire miner's son – about a tale which spread of a visit to Berenson, at I Tatti. Berenson exuded special pleasure that Moore was visiting him just at that moment, because – 'come along and see it in the library' – he had a surprise, a hitherto – look! – unknown or unattributed figure carved by Donatello. 'It isn't,' objected Moore politely, 'by Donatello.' Why not? 'It couldn't be.' Buy why? 'It's not right.' And the sculptor, who had folded his senses around every known carving by Donatello since his student days as a Rome scholar, wasn't to be shifted by the connoisseur, who produced the documentation.

'It's not right.'

More recently when H.M. was at last, so to say disgracefully at last, given a major exhibition in Paris, a neighbour of mine in Loir-et-Cher, the metal sculptor Louis Leygue, was present when two French art officials were discussing with Moore the arrangement of the exhibits. He told me that one of these two officials said to H.M. that he must be 'gratified' by having a Paris exhibition at last.

Approaching eighty, Henry Moore's reply was 'I am not a beginner, Monsieur.'

17 – THE CAFÉ ROYAL

Until the late Thirties, until the early season of the war, we still had
in London the brasserie of the Café Royal. By all accounts it wasn't
the Café Royal that it had been in the era of Sickert and Orpen and
George Moore and Wilson Steer and William Rothenstein. All the
same, you could revolve the doors from Regent Street, cross the
carpeted foyer, skip the grill room, still the haunt of elders with
money, and settle down with only cash enough for coffee and a drink
or two, in the large red brasserie, finding yourself in a very mixed
population of the famous and the obscure. Round the walls, under
the mirrors you could eat without the distaste that assailed your more
delicate senses in the vulgarity of Lyons Corner House; or with more
privacy you could eat upstairs on the surrounding balcony floor.
Baedeker of the time or a few years earlier (18th revised edition,
1923) gave the Café Royal a star and called it 'an artistic and
Bohemian rendezvous' – the only one of its kind in that grand capital
city of the world, Baedeker might have added, if you were in the
know.

Faithful to the end, painters, novelists, poets, journalists crowded
the brasserie. Among them were ghost figures out of a Ninetyish past,
such as Lord Alfred Douglas, Arthur Symons or Richard le Gal-
lienne. Had I known what he looked like, I am pretty sure I could have
identified in the brasserie that London Frenchman Valéry Larbaud –

> *Après avoir aimé des yeux dans Burlington Arcade,*
> *Je redescends Piccadilly à pied, doucement.*
> *O bouffées de printemps mêlées à des odeurs d'urine,*
> *Entre les grilles du Green Park et la station des cabs,*
> *Combien vous êtes émouvantes!*

– who wrote under a London pseudonym Barnabooth, compounded
from Barnes where he lived and Boot's at the end of his road.

Nightly habitués, older and younger, in fashion and out of fashion, included Wadsworth, Bomberg, Matthew Smith, Paul Nash, Teddy Wolfe, Epstein and his womenfolk, and Nina Hamnett, and Constant Lambert the composer. Cyril Connolly might be there, eating upstairs (downstairs wasn't his line) with authors he was going to entice down to Chelsea so that they could sign their books for him.

One or two habitués inclined to be touchy or even dangerous. It didn't do (it was one of the waiters who warned me of this) to stare in surprise at a giant of a woman, the poet Anna Wickham, author, incongruously, of a favourite anthology poem about a very wee or meek husband

> *I am a quiet gentleman*
> *And I would sit and dream;*
> *But my wife is on the hillside,*
> *Wild as a hill-stream.*

Anna Wickham would notice the unbelieving stare, take offence, stride between rows and tables and smite the offender.

The brasserie too was a refuge for political Bohemians. At an adjoining table next to my wife and myself there sat one evening Kerensky, one time head of the Russian revolutionary government, whom the Bolsheviks threw out into Europe, and Madame Kerensky. They left after a while, and Mme Kerensky left with the new black gloves my wife had bought that day. Perhaps she had been short of money to buy herself a new pair.

One of my stranger encounters in the Café was with a grey middle-aged bent man, shabbily dressed, whom I recognized soon enough as Edgar Wallace, though he never identified himself. For me it was a kind of sociological encounter, and I spent much of that late evening discovering how such a writer behaved, and what the nature was of such a best-selling author, such a famous lowbrow or middlebrow, as I should have called him then. It sounds priggish, but it is true that I humoured him and that he didn't suspect the fact when he instructed me in one way and another about, for instance, wise and foolish behaviour in the wickedness of London's West End.

I took out my pocket book which was rather stuffed with notes because I was off to Paddington on the way to Cornwall by a train after midnight. I took out a note for my bill. 'You don't know who I am,' said Edgar Wallace. 'You should be more careful. Never flash your money like that.' And he added 'Now I am going to show you a thing or two.' Protectively and educationally he took me round some dens, I suppose I should call them, below pavement level in the alleys at the back of the Café Royal. He was good company, and kind company, and I liked him. 'Remember what I've told you,' he said, holding the taxi door open when I took off for Paddington.

Equally well in the Café Royal I might have encountered an unfrocked priest or a brothel-keeper who had taken a first in Greats.

When we had come out short of money and unable to afford the Café Royal, I and my friends used to eat at a counter in a hole in the wall at the Piccadilly Circus end of Shaftesbury Avenue, where they sold first-class cups of creamy coffee and sandwiches of peppery, pink Liptauer cheese to the whores, who were everywhere around Piccadilly Circus, everywhere on the Soho side then. If you walked down Glasshouse Street, which runs more or less east and west, on a sunny evening, there was a golden glow in every doorway which sheltered a head of hair blonde from the bottle. It was rather a beautiful sight. Then, too, for a cheap meal and some of the best cooked rice imaginable, we went down some stairs of frayed lino off Denman Street into a bare room presided over by a very fat slow-moving Greek named Stelio. Greek or Cypriot restaurants, believe it or not, were uncommon still in the Thirties. They ministered to Greeks from the City, who raised their eyebrows rather at one's intrusion, but slowly became friends. In Stelio's shabby *hellenikon hestiatorion* there was no ornament except a faded photograph of the Parthenon hanging askew on the wall. There was no notice on the street up above.

The Café Royal was the thing, all the same, and the end of its brasserie as an 'artistic and Bohemian rendezvous' left London centreless in a fashion, contributing more than you would think, and just at a wrong time, to something of a new provinciality, which offset a growing sophistication and consciousness, in the arts, I mean. The closure, when it came, made for a lack of confidence in our own cultural abilities and sufficiency, even if some of the damage was undone or the weakness strengthened by the arrival of so many artists from Germany under the Nazis. And then the war came, with a London scattering which made matters worse for a while.

As a people we were unkind or less kind than we should have been, for our own good, to the new cultural emigrés and immigrants. We were jealous and failed to keep any of the best and most creative of them, who would rather have stayed with us, on the European side of the Atlantic, had we given them the chance prestigiously and economically.

It was something to go to Herbert Read's studio in Hampstead and meet handsome tall and grave Walter Gropius, for instance, and hear him interrogating Eliot on Swift and the form and clear language of *Gulliver's Travels*, the first book he read in English during his own enforced travels; but how long was it before Gropius was lost to us and swallowed up by the more appreciative Americans?

Kokoschka stayed for a while and was fun. 'Your hair is the colour of ripe strawberries,' he said at a crowded party in Highgate, spotting a girl he did not know who had arrived late and whose hair wasn't at all the colour of ripe strawberries. 'I kiss your hand,' he continued when he reached her side, and he began with kissing her elbow and coming down her forearm kiss by kiss, until he did reach her hand. The English didn't care for Kokoschka's Viennese baroque in paint or in behaviour, and thought it an odd thing to do (as it was, from our point of view, our Hampstead leaning to Picasso and Braque) when he painted a panoramic landscape of Polperro employing all the tricks of his Viennese manner. We never felt at ease with him, and he never felt at home with us, I would say, though he became an English citizen. The stiffness of some of the Germans and other central Europeans never relaxed, and I recall formal half-frozen evenings, for instance with Moholy-Nagy and his wife in Golders Green where emigré guests, who had once had to do with the Bauhaus, sat in their black suits and drank and talked a little too solemnly.

Anyhow it wasn't long before Moholy had gone, and was being firmly established by dollars in his Institute of Design at Chicago.

Maybe that the Americans who were so ready to pay for them, needed the German art emigrés more than we did in those years, on our fringe of Europe. I believe one of the few distinguished scholars from Germany to whom – was it Oxford, was it Cambridge? – gave a post was a classicist.

One small item in this settlement, such as it was, afforded some pleasurable irony. I had as neighbour in Keats Grove towards the end of my time there the small sprightly emigré artist Fred Uhlmann, who illustrated a booklet I wrote about the Isles of Scilly, which were much visited by painters when Europe and its stimulus were denied them. Other painters to be encountered there, profiting by the marvellous light of the Islands, were, with Fred Uhlmann in their wake, John Craxton, and his friend Lucien Freud, and that elder and instructor who belonged to John Piper's generation and my own, Graham Sutherland.

Now that emigré artist had an English wife, and an English father-in-law; and that artist – think of it, an artist – was not merely an exile from Germany, he was a German-Jewish exile; and that German-Jewish or Jewish-German artist's wife's father and his father-in-law was not only a general and an MP, not only a Tory aristocrat with a castle, he was a minster of the crown about to become a peer, and one of the extreme right known to be or suspected of being not without sympathy for Nazis and Fascists: he was Sir Henry Page-Croft, of Croft Castle in the county of Herefordshire, Under-secretary of State for War. Ironic justice, surely.

18 – CYRIL CONNOLLY

Why has he thrown Conscience, like a dead rat,
to putrefy in the well?

Sloth rots the intelligence

It does not do to name your animals after your friends. I had once a cat named Ben, after Ben Nicholson (who was a fancier of cats). Ben did not think the bestowal of that name quite right, quite proper, as if it had been a touch almost of lese-majesty, not against him, but against painting. Ben the Cat was a silver tabby. I explained to Ben the Artist that the relationship – the exquisite relationship of the silver and grey tones in some of his pictures, especially in one of a hand of playing cards which I owned, was repeated in the grey and silver striped fur of Ben the Cat. Ben wasn't exactly pleased, all the same, and dropped the subject, and I took care not to address the cat any more as Ben, in Ben's presence.

We had a donkey which we named Basil after Basil Taylor, but this time only to Basil's slightly and affectionately amused dismay. Still, each of the Basils possessed undeniable charm and good looks, and each of them was undeniably obstinate. Basil the Donkey could never be persuaded across a small stream near the house, which wasn't deep enough to have wetted his hooves, and the other Basil was obstinate in the rightness of his estimate of the character of certain artists, museum directors, pretentious poets, and the like.

Then as well we owned a war-time pig, fattening slowly at the back of the garage and awaiting the knife, to be transformed into cutlets and chops and crackling.

He was astonishingly like Cyril Connolly, so we called him Cyril.

Cyril the Critic, in his own style, was an ugly man, there is no denying. His pig-likeness upset him, I am sure, and could be held responsible for a certain smart ugliness in his character, a rebuffing quality, affecting his literary likes and dislikes. Stories were told about him, sometimes stories about his appearance, sometimes stories exemplifying his wit and the sharpness of his mind and tongue, but never, my recollection would be, lovable stories. It went round that after a lunch at the Ivy on a foggy day Cyril and A. J. Ayer the philosopher, Freddie Ayer, apparently went their separate and opposite ways, disappearing into the fog, in which Ayer was discussing the unpleasantness of Cyril. Out of the fog behind him came a voice, Cyril's voice, 'Not so loud, Freddie. Not so loud.' And hadn't Ayer once said that Cyril wasn't as nice as he looked?

Cyril was cruel, entertainingly cruel, with his tongue. Some of his grand hostesses, who liked to be in the literary fashion, were afraid of him on that score, afraid that at another great house he might talk about them as they had encouraged him to talk so wittily – there was no doubting the wit – about others. But they would invite him all the same, to liven up their house parties.

Gossip said he was as cruel with his hand as with his tongue – cruel, I mean, to his women. Oliver Simon the typographer who printed Cyril's magazine *Horizon*, went round very early one morning to Cyril's flat in Russell Square with urgently required proofs. The door was not locked and he went in and waited, after ringing the bell. Through the bathroom door then came a noise of slapping, then a noise of weeping, and more slapping and weeping and sobbing.

The bathroom door opened and Cyril emerged, in a silk dressing-gown (real silk, I am sure and as likely as not still unpaid for).

'We have been naughty,' he said. 'We needed punishment. Ah, Oliver, the proofs. Good.'

Oliver handed over the proofs, and left, the sobs dying away on the other side of the door into the bathroom where Cyril's girl had been punished.

This short, plump, ugly Old Etonian, who carried a butterfly net for the capture of genius, was and needed to be a good host. Norman Cameron and I, one evening in Norman's flat in the Fulham Road, persuaded Dylan Thomas into a clean shirt, and a clean tie, not spotted with food, and brushed and spruced him up to go to a dinner with Cyril in the King's Road, at which the genius from Swansea and the London pubs was to be launched and introduced to various litterateurs, among them the still very active Desmond MacCarthy, who was certainly romantic about genius – of a kind.

Dylan was scared, as he often was, Dylan was uncertain of how to manipulate knife and fork. Not altogether free of the effects of his last drinking of beer in the Fulham Road, he began filling up once more and gaining courage and telling old dirty chestnuts which Cyril and his guests had known from childhood.

The launch was not a success, though genius could be forgiven, and its eccentricities excused. That, I am sure, is how Cyril Connolly carried off the evening without embarrassment.

I speak of Cyril as a person, when you met him, and inspected him, and suspected his nastier, crueller, wittier, smarter traits as the consequence of slights visited on him in childhood. He had his own to hold and to develop among others – other writers, I mean – of a like nature.

He and Evelyn Waugh were friends and two prime exemplars, talented yet detestable, who *knew*, and yet in action and opinion often denied; offensive often to the creative purities of art. Evelyn Waugh, I realised from direct report, if not direct experience, he being high on my short list of celebrated authors I never wanted to meet or have dealings with, was capable of shocking nastiness to those who were mild and inoffensive and incapable of answering back, let alone of acting in kind. I have been told that Evelyn Waugh's father, the publisher Arthur Waugh, spoke with a poor command of the King's English and was decidedly, if a successful publisher, 'no gentleman'. That could illuminate traits in the character – and the writing – of his eminent son, who I would dare to say if you take his pages inch by inch, was far from a master of fresh and lively English, adept in manipulating clichés, but not in recognizing them. One of the poets I knew – I think Charles Madge – talked disdainfully of those who were found out as writers and fell back on being gentlemen. Equally there is always a supply of those who when found out as gentlemen fall back on being writers.

Perhaps Connolly too was victim of a certain chagrin at being in fact Irish and not English. He saw plenty of Ireland in his childhood (in which he confessed to having been 'a little vicious golden-haired Caligula'), and must have known that every second butcher's shop in Ireland has Connolly (if not MacCarthy) over the door. His Irish father, it was true, was in the English army, and had made a good marriage, but he had risen no higher than a major. Perhaps the social ethos in which Connolly grew up – with Eton to help – can be detected in Major Connolly's one, anonymous, contribution to our literature, a pamphlet *Pottery, by a Potter*, on 'Home made Potted Foods, Meat and Fish Pastes, Savoury Butters and Others'. The foreword to that pamphlet talks about the second and third kitchen-maids (whose fingers did the potting) and the Good Old Days and how the array of servants used to file into the dining-room for morning prayers; and Major Connolly dealt in such words as *yclept* and *spicy treat* and *veriest gourmet*, suggesting, excellent as the recipes are, more than the culinary taste of the Connollys.

This scholar of Eton and Brackenbury Scholar of Balliol, this Chevalier de la Légion d'Honneur, this member of Pratt's and White's, had much, it appears, to make him act superior and feel inferior all at the same time.

How avid he was, in rather an old-fashioned way, to collect both authors and association copies of their books. Once in the Café Royal, he found Auden, Isherwood and myself and Stephen Spender. He whisked us upstairs to eat and then whisked us down to Chelsea. Auden and Isherwood and Spender were not so well known then. They were young, but Cyril had his eye on them – as on Dylan Thomas. And they hadn't been sitting five minutes in Cyril's quarters before, to their surprise he was out with the books they had published up to date, asking for their signatures.

What I found unpleasant in Connolly, as in the writing conduct of those who seemed to belong to his party, is that though they might judge well and write well they divided the writers of their time too much into those whose writing it was safe to praise and those whose writing it was safe (and advantageous) only to condemn or discourage. Connolly in this way found it safe and socially expedient to sneer in review after review at the books which Wyndham Lewis wrote, whereas the literary and literary-social tide seemed to be flowing too strongly in buoying up, shall I say, Eliot and Virginia Woolf, and then Auden – and then Dylan Thomas.

He knew and experienced deeply, is my judgement of Cyril Connolly, and then contradicted himself wilfully, and weakly. Keen in taste, brilliantly erudite, skilful, persuasive and witty in his smooth mandarin English, and not caring much for the human race in its situation, my verdict on Connolly, on the basis of my reading of him, and my few and not very willing direct contacts with him, is that he wasn't free, or that he was less free than most of us – surely himself included – would like to be.

How much there is to agree with, and be thankful for, in the paragraphs of his notebook *The Unquiet Grave*; for instance, that 'Complacent mental laziness is the English disease', a disease from which he never exempted himself. And how that one witticism of his which everyone knows that 'imprisoned in every fat man a thin man is wildly signalling to get out' can be accompanied by a statement that every true writer, or partly, intermittently true writer wants all the time to get clear of his inescapable fetters.

19 – BONAMY DOBRÉE

Bonamy Dobrée came of a wealthy cultured Channel Island family, a family responsible for the Dobrée Museum at Nantes, which contains far the best collection of Nottingham alabasters, a family too which was distinguished in Victorian politics. So not unnaturally Bonamy, if he ended life as a scholar and professor, began it as a professional soldier; and a very handsome one too he must have looked, with his fine features, small moustache and alert manner, his fencer's figure, like an officer – and he wasn't without a matching frivolity – in some Viennese social comedy.

This dear man, *bon ami* indeed, was one of Eliot's close friends, one of his Faber and Faber circle, and I asked him once how the soldier, the gunner and lieutenant-colonel had become the scholar and the man of letters and the professor. 'My dear Geoffrey,' was Bonamy's throwaway reply, 'when I retired from the army I didn't know what to do, so I took up literature.'

His tone was one of infinite good humour. Staying with him and his wife, who had a beauty and alertness to match, and who wrote the once celebrated novel (how good a novel?) *Your Cuckoo Sings by Kind*, I left their house outside Leeds, where this brisk military man was the Professor of English, with a cardboard box filled with rhizomes of that pale blue iris which blossoms all of a sudden in mid-winter, even in snow. Whenever those irises come into flower, I am reminded of Bonamy – of this literary ex-gunner, this Haileybury boy commissioned from Woolwich – lying for rest on our sofa after heart trouble, though in mind as sprightly as ever, handing out books he had brought with him to my young children. With those irises I began a habit of growing or trying to grow kinds of plant which had to do with authors I loved or authors who intrigued me – Viper's Bugloss (but he was no viper) for Crabbe, irises again from Balzac's *château* at Saché, off the gardener's rubbish heap, a rose, though it can have been descended only in thought from any rose that he knew, from Herrick's churchyard at Dean Prior.

The result of that floral habit might be – once certainly was – rather a comic failure. I had taken some American friends past the ponds on Hampstead Heath and up the hill to Highgate Cemetery to see the tombs of George Eliot, Wombwell the Victorian circus proprietor, on which stone tears roll down the face of a stone lion, and Karl Marx. One of the Americans picked a spray of the red rose bush ornamenting Marx's enclosure. I didn't quite approve, not on political grounds, not on anti-Russian grounds, nor on philosophic grounds, only because that rose bush would soon have been naked and moribund had every visitor robbed it in the same way.

I put that rose cutting into a tooth-mug when we got home, intending to plant it, in hopes, the next day. But next day after breakfast the gaunt Hampstead woman who charred for us stuck her head through the door and announced that she had thrown out that old withered bit of rose from the kitchen. She was given, that gaunt person, to sticking her head into the room with messages and admonitions. Once it was 'I wouldn't leave baby out in her pram like that. I worked for a lady once who left her baby out in the garden, and what do you think, a great big Alsatian came and bit the baby's head off.'

Better to pick off a flower or two *in memoriam*, sea-pinks from those North Cornish cliffs where ancient Thomas Hardy went to view a voiceless ghost, kingcups from the edge of Thomas Hardy's Stour,

> *Closed were the kingcups and the mead*
> *Dripped in monotonous green,*

or perhaps a bunch of Donne's huge primroses, which still, as in his poem, ornament the path up to Montgomery Castle.

To return, though, to Bonamy. Herbert Read, Bonamy and I were discussing what new poets – unknown and little-known poets and poems, that is – should go into the *London Book of English Verse* the two of them were preparing. I urged them to include something by

Swift's protégé William Diaper, whom I had just discovered with excitement.

'The trouble with you, Geoffrey,' said Bonamy, when I quoted

> And earth looks pale on the declining moon,

'is that you can always find the one good line in a bad poet.' Specialist as he was in eighteenth-century literature, Bonamy had never heard of Diaper, or noticed or followed up the scornful mention of him in Pope's *Dunciad*. But how quickly he made amends, and set one of his Ph.D. students to prepare, at last, an edition of Diaper (which Herbert and I were able to include in the new *Muses Library*).

Bonamy was a scholar with an open mind, a mind he could make up for himself, and a generous mind too. He liked the idea that Diaper, a poor curate who died young, before he had gathered friends enough around him to float his memory, should at last have an edition to himself, should at last, and deservedly, join the long roll of good minor poets.

The admirable Dublin poet John Winstanley (also I think, known to Swift) and the mysterious Edward May, of Trinity College, Cambridge –

> *Behold, my dearest, how the fragrant rose*
> *Is fresh and blown, whilst on the tree it grows;*
> *But being by some rude hand pluck'd away,*
> *Loseth its sweetness, and doth soon decay:*
> *Even so poor I, or live, or die by thee,*
> *I am thy rose, my dear, and thou my tree*

– were other poets, I think, Bonamy would have wished to restore to memory.

A question occurs to me, thinking both of Bonamy Dobrée and Herbert Read. Were they taken in – yes, 'taken in' is still my conviction and expression – by Dylan Thomas? Others weren't. Eliot wasn't, though he might have excused himself by insisting, as he often did, how more and more difficult it becomes to judge poetry by those who are much younger than oneself. Auden wasn't. Edwin

Muir was, but then Edwin was rather a simple and romantic soul. I have not searched through the printed opinions on this subject – this tender subject – either by Bonamy or Herbert; but from what I recall of their conversation I think at the most they were only half taken in. They were not Americans. Or neo-Romantics.

20 – READING 'ANTIQUITY'

I should like to have you tell me why Browne's Urn
Makes all the past with firework colours burn.
                                        Wyndham Lewis

When I was thinking about the magazines of my time, the literary
magazines, the weeklies and the book pages, I happened to come on
a letter which the young Tolstoy wrote long long ago to his older
friend V. P. Botkin the critic crying out for a new journal. It was
1858. Everyone was caught up, pro and con, evasive, undecided, in
the problem and prospects of emancipation. A 'sordid stream of
politics' engulfed everything and threatened to destroy or defile art,
so how would it be if Turgenev, Botkin, Fet the poet and himself
joined in the production of a journal proclaiming the 'independence
and eternity of art', saving art from politics, attracting all that is
purely artistic on its own, teaching the public and not imitating the
public's taste; not trying 'to prove anything or know anything,' not
trying to know about this or that trend, and having 'one aim, artistic
enjoyment – tears and laughter?'

'The periodical of Utopia'. Could it ever exist? Could it have
existed then?

Even in Moscow in 1858 could enough have been found, issue by
issue, to achieve that grand aim of tears and laughter on that level of
the independence and the eternity of art (which eternity in 1984
everyone would deny)? Botkin and Turgenev, we are told, were
against it. They were older than Tolstoy, and had a worldlier sense,
no doubt.

Has there ever been an English or American literary periodical of
that kind or near it in the past sixty years, with an exalted enough
programme? The *Dial?* The *Little Review? Blast? The Criterion?*
transition? I think not. Every shrewd editor – and there have been
several shrewd editors – trims a little, slips a little, inserts elements of

cocktail into his editing. Every good editor needs an axe to grind, even if the axe is unlikely to have the edge and shine of Tolstoy's intention. Every good editor feels an exultancy. Eliot's *Criterion* should have been this century's influencer. I held it in awe, as an undergraduate. Eliot could entice contributions which looked over the confines of Russell Square into the other countries of Europe. But Eliot niggled, and Eliot was not Tolstoy's little finger. Thought, in the well designed pages of the *Criterion*, was not always disturbing in the better way; covert politics slightly defiled its superiority. Wonderful as it was to be asked to write in the *Criterion*, even at the back end, I can't say that Eliot's review, since he was not that kind of editor or that kind of complete man or complete mind, ever glowed with an infectious healthiness of art.

Looking back and cross-examining myself now for the magazine the contents of which I once felt as an influence liberating and uplifting, I know that I should mention *Cahiers d'Art*. Each of its huge issues (bought in Anton Zwemmer's bookshop in Charing Cross Road, that vital station of London's intellectualism of the late 1920s and the 1930s, of which I write on another page) unlocked and lavishly exhibited secret gardens of world art, at a time when the English elect, conventionally, were held to be Augustus John and Wilson Steer and Dame Laura Knight. *Cahiers d'Art* was the great eye-opener; it was divine visual food for those so long on a dull diet, in that business of the eternity of art, provided by the political, semi-literary, semi-cultural weeklies, or by the *London Mercury*.

I belonged to a family of brothers who avidly read the *New Statesman*. We would walk five miles for it by footpaths to the Fowey River, cross by the ferry to a small W. H. Smith's in Fowey which we associated otherwise with Quiller-Couch of *Troy Town* and the *London Mercury* (W. H. Smith nowadays in my neighbouring towns of Swindon and Marlborough and Cirencester and Chippenham doesn't 'carry', as they say, the *Statesman* or *The Times Literary Supplement*), and then walk home again to our Cornish vicarage with that treasure of the week. But the literary end of the *Statesman* and of the other weeklies, semi-political and semi-literary, was not scintillating. Only the *New Republic* of those years, from New York, seemed alive and expectant at either end, surprising my young American wife and myself and our friends with its lack of provinciality, its active seriousness about literature, and its frequent publication, a page at a time, of poems by poets we wanted to know about. It was better designed and printed as well.

All the same, even the *New Republic*, in that splendid period of its existence, came under the curse, as I see it still, which ordains that most literary journalism in our language must be for ever mixed with politics, whether of the foreshore or the backwoods. I could not say I was influenced in my depths by the periodicals I have mentioned – *Cahiers d'Art* excepted (but then I was a friend of painters, though not a painter). My periodical, as it turned out, was not literary at all. On those journeys to fetch a *New Statesman* from Fowey we passed a manorial pound, a mill which had been grinding in the thirteenth century and an Iron Age enclosure, and we crossed a field of Bronze Age barrows where I picked up flint arrowheads, and once an armorial button which had fallen from the livery coat of some retainer of the Buller family.

One magazine would relate all these things, including, if not the button with the Saracen's head, certainly the ancient path by which it was found, and that one magazine *Antiquity*, founded, and edited then, by O. G. S. Crawford, still seems to have been the flower of all periodicals familiar to me. Few non-literary periodicals can ever have been so stimulating to the literary imagination as that quarterly dealing with the past, rather as the past was understood by Marc Bloch in France, and later by W. G. Hoskins in England. And how professional it looked, how appetisingly it was laid out and printed (by John Bellows, the Quaker printer in Gloucester, who was a friend of Tolstoy's, and an expert on Roman Gloucester).

Crawford – I never met him, though I had sharp impatient letters from him, from this always inquisitive cultured man, whose patience was not increased by ignorance or foolish enquiry or sham archæology such as Stonehenge evoked, and still evokes – can accurately be described as enlightened, enthusiastic, polymathic, sceptical, imaginative, and aloof. *Antiquity* belonged to him. This magazine began, he wrote in one issue, 'as the private venture of a particular person, but he could never have started it if he had not felt that others beside himself needed an organ to express their point of view and to publish the cream of their researches.'

Contributors sensed what Crawford wanted from them, and supplied it, authority and interest, without either unsupported generalization or too many and too complex professional data. This field archæologist of our British Isles, and of the world also, held human diversity and change and unity in his focus. Each number of his quarterly review was an excitement, concentrated in an article, it might be on the Uffington White Horse, or the travels of the Celtic saints, or fortified churches in Transylvania, or megaliths in Assam, or the origins of cultivated plants, or water-clocks, or Cornish fish cellars, or the Cerne Giant, that flasher of Dorset, or querns, or roses in antiquity.

This educated imaginative editor assumed that his readers would see life and the past in the same way as he did himself. He expected them to enjoy plainness in his editorial notes – 'Planning is naturally repugnant to many people' (prolegomenon to a charge that no adequate map of the Roman Empire existed). 'Only in the heart of the British Empire is it necessary on each separate occasion when the need arises, to bring public opinion to bear on lethargy.'

This editor hated ignorance when it presumed, and slapped it down, but I think he must have been glad that his *Antiquity* had so many readers who were not prehistorians or historians. Like Sir Thomas Browne, in the words of Wyndham Lewis's poem, this adventure of a particular person made 'the past with firework colours burn' – that was so for me, at any rate, giving me a sense that man's earth was for ever simultaneously old and young, lucid and obscure or opaque.

Antiquity under O. G. S. Crawford, who edited it from 1927 until 1957, when he died, has reminded me of another poet, Samuel Daniel: it seemed, as Daniel wrote of literature,

to combine in one
All ages past, and make one live with all,

enabling me, I feel, to

confer with who are gone
And the dead living unto councell call.

That was something, providing the *mise en scène* of the eternity of art, say what we will nowadays.

Reading them through I find Daniel's lines a memoir of the mind – of the recent mind – for many more surely than myself. Change the terms, too, but not the milieu altogether, and wouldn't Crawford be proffering an apt programme for a poet's duties and occupation? There he was, and how refreshing in a self-advertising era, pushing ideas and possibilities forward, but himself never. Imagine this O. G. S. Crawford pontificating on television.

Antiquity was an archaeologists' *Criterion*. I have to think that O. G. S. Crawford was archaeology's Eliot, that without the unlikely aid of a quixotic multi-millionaire now and again, we are going to be given no more private ventures of particular persons, no more plump and helpful magazines of good writing, any that are left rapidly dwindling into tiresome amateur 'little magazines'.

There will be no Joe Ackerleys, no George Barneses, manipulating, or being allowed to manipulate, or wanting to manipulate public money in old-fashioned literary ways, of which the essence is independence.

Milch ewes which were plump, dwindle and die after a few years, making no mutton and needing no shot from a humane killer. The corpses often rot on the deserted hills, and the dry bones lie about on the grass.

21 – HOMES AND GRAVES

Recently, after a long interval, I went a third time to visit the stone laid above Henry Vaughan under a yew tree in Llansantffraed church yard outside Brecon, and for the third time I found flowers at one end of the stone fading in an old green-grown jam jar. Who puts them there? The same person every time, some Brecon Welshman or Anglo-Welshman still remembering him, in love with his poems, and moved by the inscription, which was his own choice –

> *Servus Inutilis:*
> *Peccator Maximus*
> *Hic Jaceo?*

I admit it is absurd to go visiting the graves of poets and artists, seeing how our convictions about death and an afterlife have changed. I do it, all the same; I admit, as well to my own surreptitious placing of flowers, wild ones as a rule, on such gravestones or memorials, excusing myself by a self-assurance that the visit and the flowers make me realize all the more that the art of the dead is alive.

I have visited George Herbert's church at Bemerton in Wiltshire, where his burial is marked only by a stone which is set diamond-wise in the chancel floor and is inscribed only with the initial G. H.; and to balance that I look around another Wiltshire church, the extra noble priory church of Edington, remembering that Herbert was married there.

I have been – but then who hasn't – to Stoke Poges, on account of Gray's *Elegy*, if not on account of anything else to do with Gray who doesn't seem to have been the warmest of men; and to Grasmere on account – that's better – of Wordsworth and as much or more on account of Dorothy Wordsworth. I have been to what little there is of the Abbey of Strata Florida in Wales because in its graveyard the monks laid the body of Dafydd ap Gwilym, also to the church – the still existing medieval church of Llanbadarn in which Dafydd ap Gwilym in his poem 'Merched Llanbadarn', 'The Ladies of Llanbadarn', says he was jeered at *sotto voce* by the girls on Sunday. In Somerset I have been to Beckinton church to read the wall-side stone of Samuel Daniel, Shakespeare's friend, because he wrote, in *Musophilus*, of virtue, the work of doing well, that

> *over looks the base, contemptible,*
> *And low-laid follies of mortalitie,*

of

> *blessed letters that combine in one*
> *All ages past, and make one live with all,*

by which

> *we do confer with who are gone,*
> *And the dead living unto councell call,*

who spoke of knowledge as the soul of the world, ejaculating

> *what good is like to this,*
> *To do worthy the writing, and to write*
> *Worthy the reading, and the world's delight.*

In Oxfordshire, too, what a profitable experience or instigation of thought and emotions it is to look down in Kelmscott churchyard on the long stone covering what remained of that secular saint and neglected poet William Morris; in the Isle of Wight to find at Bonchurch Swinburne's grave above the sea which waved and swayed in his also neglected and now underesteemed verses. In France more of pilgrimaging than rubber-necking has taken me to Valéry's grave, Valéry's modest share of the white family tomb above the Mediterranean at Sète, in the glittering *cimetière marin* of his poem, to Ronsard's tomb beside the Loire at Tours, to Millet's overgrown, altogether neglected memorial which crumbles, national monument or not, in the churchyard near Barbizon.

It seems to me that the French are less inclined to – what shall I say, semi-aesthetic or touristical semi-aesthetic, semi-art-appreciative rubber-necking than ourselves (or the Americans), that they are more given – I hope so – to looking at the pictures and reading the poems and the books; which brings Monet to mind. I travelled to the Eure to report on the restoration of Monet's garden of water-lilies and irises and roses at Giverny, and thought I should climb first into the churchyard where he was buried above his house, his great studio and his garden. The French acknowledge his supremacy of genius. But what did I find there? A special gravestone? A tall monument?

No, simply the classic, healthiest example of French mortuary neglect, a brief inscription around an ill-designed white memorial commemorating various obscure members of his wife's family.

What I would say has been of more profit to me than visiting graves, though the two so often go together, is visiting or soaking myself for a while in scenery spiritualized, I suppose that is the word, by writers in their poems, the Quantocks for Coleridge, the Lakes even more obviously for Wordsworth and his sister, the Cotswolds for Ivor Gurney, the Vale of Clwyd for Hopkins, Long Island (wiping it clean again in fancy to the nakedness and the sands and sea birds he knew) for Walt Whitman, and then, outside Brecon once more, the Black Mountains, rivers, streams and waterfalls and the Llangorse Lake, recognizable in Vaughan's verbal spiritualization of the scenery he had known since childhood.

There are discoveries to be made in this way. Searching the map, I found that there exists a neglected waterfall just outside Brecon which Vaughan might have had in mind when he wrote his waterfall poem. Had he translated the Welsh name of the stream, which is Ffrwdgrech, into the 'loud brook' of his poem? That could be the meaning of the Welsh in these Ffrwdgrech Falls. So I looked for the waterfall, to which there is no path, which can be missed on a lane which doesn't give a hint of the Falls' existence; and I felt as if I were the first person to recognize the falls and admire their extraordinary charm since Vaughan had been there repeatedly in his seventeenth century.

In France, again, isn't there a spiritualization of the Vendômois and its ivy-hung wine caves and wide water-meadows in Ronsard's poems; and in his essays of the country immediately around the Château de Montaigne in the Dordogne and the tower in which Montaigne sat and thought and wrote, in the orchards, the meadows, the valley immediately below the terrace of the *château*, and the way the sun strikes the *château* walls and the sides of his valley?

In Germany isn't the purity of sane and mad Hölderlin accented in that sad tower he inhabited above the Neckar, at Tübingen?

Belleslettrism, dilettantism, all of this? Old-fashioned belleslettrism? If you like. But we exist, writer and reader, painter and collector and haunter of art galleries, in this world of our sensations, not in a vacuum.

Gravestones, memorials, can be disgusting, too. For years, though I loved him and his poems, I never went near the churchyard at Helpston where John Clare is buried. Going there at last, how it disgusted and infuriated me to find that his memorial, in the most well-meaning, yet most patronizing way, calls him 'the Peasant Poet'.

Clare left a sketch among his papers of the gravestone he wanted –the simplest of stones, rough hewn, and on it

HERE
Rest the
HOPES
and Ashes
of
John Clare

But that wouldn't do.

22 — GEOFFREY TAYLOR

Let Easter Eggs with double yolk
Bear Helen and Emanuel

In Ireland – maybe in England too – has everyone forgotten Geoffrey Taylor, of whom I have read only a single account, and that an account which is far from just, in Martin Seymour Smith's book about Robert Graves? But then the Irish are rather odd about themselves, or about Irish writers, quickly neglecting them after death unless they have been made a fuss of in England or America. And in a perverse way they will also claim as Irish, entirely Irish, some writer that we all hold in common respect, who may have had an Irish grandmother who lived in Hampstead or Bloomsbury.

In hopes of finding something about my friend Geoffrey Taylor, I have just looked through a newly published handbook or encyclopedia about the various practitioners of all the arts in Ireland, north and south. Not a word. And not a word about him under his original or proper name, which was Geoffrey Phipps. (It surprised me, incidentally, that this new encyclopedia, which has plenty to say about Beckett and *Waiting for Godot*, can't spare a word for William Allingham, let alone Geoffrey Phipps or Geoffrey Taylor, as if in childhood no Irishman was ever nourished by love of Allingham's 'Up the airy mountain, down the rushy glen').

Geoffrey Taylor – Geoffrey Phipps – who did become a contributor to *New Verse*, by the way – was born in 1900, which makes him more or less of the age of his friends Robert Graves and Ben Nicholson, and he died in 1957. Coming from a family of the English ascendancy, he spoke posh, as they say, even exceptionally posh, and his tastes were posh as well. His father sent him as Geoffrey Phipps, from Galway to that English public school of military foundation, that incubator of occasional rebels, Wellington College. When he was sixteen and the Easter uprising took place in Dublin, Geoffrey walked about in the morning with a shamrock in his buttonhole, for which his form mates put his head under a pump. When de Valera came to power, Geoffrey went to tea with him, for which his father disinherited him (so from then on he called himself Geoffrey Taylor after his Taylor relations, of Castle Taylor, now demolished, near his own Galway home). When during the war he was drinking sherry before dinner as a guest of the British High Commissioner in Dublin, Sir John Maffey, John Betjeman the Press Officer thought up one of his acts of amused roguery. To the British Military Attaché, an amiable if ordinary and conventional mortal, he said he must meet that tall thin man over there, a distinguished Irishman who was an old Wellingtonian and had once been in the British Army. The introduction made, John slipped away, but not out of hearing. 'They tell me you were once in the British Army, Mr Taylor. Jolly good show, jolly good show.'

Silence for a second or two. Then firmly, curtly, but without rancour, being always a polite man, Geoffrey bent towards the British major, and said 'Yes – yes indeed. I wore your damned khaki for a day, and took it off and deserted, and came back to my native country, where I have been, with intervals, ever since.'

Before I was due to meet Geoffrey for the first time, on the railway platform at Dublin, he had written that I must look out for the two ugliest people in Ireland. It is true that his wife at that time, the painter Nora McGuiness, was one of the last North European unfortunates to have a face which had been made rugose by smallpox, all being well, though, when she smiled. How far Geoffrey's face was rightly described as ugly can be seen from the fresh, calm portrait of him by William Nicholson, Ben Nicholson's father (William Nicholson and Geoffrey were the closest of friends), which is reproduced in Lillian Browse's book on William Nicholson, a likeness of accuracy.

He was a gay poet, and a witty one. One of the best of his few slight books *A Dash of Garlic*, printed for him, seventy-five copies only, by Ella Noyes and Nancy Nicholson, Ben's sister, who once upon a time was wife to Robert Graves, was dedicated to William Nicholson with a touch of his peculiarity and unexpectedness –.

To W.N.
An eminent painter of Blokes
Who cannot resist making jokes
With points so refined
They dawn on the mind
Quick as oak-apples grow into oaks.

If the best of the little that can be found in print of Geoffrey's verse is wit and fun, if his single famous poem is the short one about the cat Sally, inhabitant of the Nicholson household at Sutton Veney, who swallowed cheese and puffed down the holes the scented breeze, and so enticed with scented breath

'Nice mice to an untimely death',

Geoffrey thought and felt and lived through his senses:

Lapwings call, light
Leverets bound,
And Mare's-tails push thin ancient heads above the
April ground.

But then back in the Twenties Geoffrey was writing

Poetry may deal with knowledge or imagination fact
or fiction
But to cleanse that Augean stable we've got to pitch
poetic thought after poetic diction

– and in 1933 he ended *A Dash of Garlic* by saying he walked precariously on a rock-ridge

Patched poetically
With wet seaweed.

There tearing his finger-nails badly, he clung

To actuality
In the midst of laughter.

Perpetual curiosity about everything equipped him with images for thought, laughter, sharpness, tenderness.

A self-respecting tape-worm would disown you,

– who was he thinking of? –

A blow-fly'd blush to think she might have
blown you.

Eliot – he did not care for Eliot, for his cautious mandarin qualities – would

stay the swine of Gadara
With strings of imitation pearls.

Why should D. H. Lawrence have so soon retired with all his passion

To kiss his own cold shadow on the moon?

How should we get on if we were to discover that Helen of Troy had pink eyes, or if an old papyrus

More than usually informorant
Proved dove of Blessed Trinity truly a cormorant?

He insisted to me that all the poems in his first book *Withering of the Fig Leaf* were 'bluddy awful' (it was published in 1927 by Leonard and Virginia Woolf, appearing with no author's name, or rather with the name Geoffrey Phipps inked out on the title page of every copy, and the book was suppressed, though he gave me a copy). But then what was really suppressible about such a poem as 'Love'?

Write about Apollo she said
Or about the Yellow Cups she said
Or about the First Swallow she said
Or about Wine she said
And I bowed my head
And glanced in the glass preparatory to writing
about Apollo
Thinking could I kill a bird and a girl with
one rhyme
I'd drink wine from yellow cups another time

But suddenly Write about Love she said
Instead
Then I seizing chance by the forelock withdrew
  my glance from Apollo
Shall I write about Love I said
Come to bed.

There was nothing from the queerest quirk of behaviour, human or animal, from a rare or common beetle, from the history of the lawn-mower and the cutting of grass, or the history of some favourite garden flower, incapable of stirring Geoffrey's curiosity – a curiosity often which something you told him would also stir him to instant action. I told him one day at lunch in his summer garden about fritters of elder blossom and acacia blossom. Lunch was interrupted at once, a batter was made and bits of some of the edible plants in the garden – rosemary was one of them – were at once soaked and fried and sugared. Books, too, would arrive in Wiltshire from Dublin – books of Irish verse he was sure I had never encountered and equally sure I would enjoy, books which made me suppose that Dublin had the most exciting of bookstalls, which may have been true then, so many mansions having been half destroyed or deserted, but certainly isn't true now. One such book, rarely met with I suppose outside libraries, was Allingham's 'Modern Poem', *Laurence Bloomfield in Ireland*, of 1864, his story poem of the evictions in Ireland, a poem which Geoffrey Taylor – but who else? – knew had been much admired by Turgenev. And Geoffrey and Turgenev were right about its quality and interest.

Was Geoffrey the kind of writer nowadays referred to a little derisively or contemptuously as a 'man-of-letters', a kind of literary dodo? – though he was a tall thin moa – no, a tall slender egret or flamingo – and not a fat dumpy waddling dodo.

I find it sad and not easily explicable that no collected edition of his poems has ever been published. He must have left many poems behind, and I wouldn't think that Ireland – or England – should forget him. Perhaps he was too sharp for some:

I detest barrel-organs hate barrel-organs loathe their
noise and I think Mount Parnassus
A proper place for growing wild oats to feed tame asses.

Geoffrey Taylor is far from the only Irish poet whom the Irish have allowed to slip into oblivion, as if, let me say once more, the necessary test was whether and how far their poems have succeeded with the English.

What I should have emphasized is that Geoffrey's obscurity as a poet was really Geoffrey's own fault. I did mention that he suppressed his first book *Withering of the Fig Leaf*, after seeing to it that 'Geoffrey Phipps' was indelibly blotted out on the title page, without any substitution of 'Geoffrey Taylor', and that *A Dash of Garlic* was limited to seventy-five copies. I should have added that the authorship of *A Dash of Garlic* was indicated only by the initials G.T., and that the third, intervening collection, *It was not Jones* (Hogarth Living Poets No. 2, Hogarth Press, 1928), was ascribed to a mythical 'R. Fitzurse'.

So after all could even the most fervent of Irish literary patriots be blamed for knowing nothing of a poet who suppressed one book, which crept into the world with no name on cover or title page, and set only his initials on another, and only a pseudonym on the intervening one? And that intervening book as long ago, or rather as early as 1928, contained one poem in praise of Eluard and another headed 'Picasso's Pink Period on the Virginals' when there were not so many English poets or Irish poets who had ever heard of Eluard or ever set eyes on a Picasso.

23 – ANTHOLOGIES

*To those who, like myself, take pleasure
in anthologies . . .*

T. S. Eliot

When Robert Graves and Laura Riding, that bluestocking whom so
many have never known how to take or tackle, published their
Pamphlet against Anthologies in 1928, they certainly helped forward a
revolution, though I would rather say a reformation, in poetry, or in
the taste for poetry. That was all of fifty-six years ago and their
pamphlet came out when I had just ceased to be an undergraduate.
Of the Oxford poets Auden had ended his last year at Christ Church,
Louis MacNeice had still three years to go at Merton, and Stephen
Spender three years at University College, but the Oxford revolution, if it can be called so, was already in progress. Louis had by now
published his first book of poems, his rather Sitwellian – Edith
Sitwellian – *Blind Fireworks*, and in this 1928 Cecil Day Lewis, fresh
from Wadham, began with his still rather Georgian *Country Comets*.

Coming at this time the Riding-Graves pamphlet – a thickish
pamphlet it was – made for scepticism and caution and a dismissal of
poems about lambs, and of poetical lachrymosity. Gardens were out.
'A garden is a lovesome thing, God wot!' – the anthological career of
that famous piece was over, or nearly over. Its anthological
companion piece 'O blackbird, what a boy you are' also began its
passage into oblivion. The only anthologies we permitted ourselves
to like were *The Spirit of Man* – good title, good theme – chosen by
Robert Bridges (who was Poet Laureate), and then, with reser-
vations, *The Golden Treasury*, which had done service since 1864,
and Walter de la Mare's *Come Hither*. On those three I would say that
all children in literate middle-class and upper-class families were
brought up, though I have asked myself whether *The Golden Treasury*
would ever have been so accepted, had the name on spine and title-

130

page been Cohen, the family name which Palgrave's father had jettisoned for so political and romantic and knightly a patronym. (*The Golden Treasury*, chosen by Meyer Cohen? No.)

A poet had been responsible not only for *The Spirit of Man* and *Come Hither*, but also for much of *The Golden Treasury* – Tennyson, than whom few poets ever had a more subtle ear, having helped his friend Palgrave to draw up the lists, and having (I think) invented the title.

That was an extenuation, whereas Riding and Graves were beginning to feel hemmed in by anthologies which anybody in the trade had chosen, poetaster, hack or publisher, or all three in one.

Riding and Graves had induced a healthy fear, a hesitation. I felt as much, and showed as much in 1939 when Eliot, who was to publish it, advised me about the first anthology I put together, a choice of the poems which had been printed in *New Verse*, of which the last number had just been published. 'You seem doubtful,' said Eliot. I mentioned Riding and Graves. 'Nonsense,' said Eliot, or words to that effect, nonsense being a downright expletive he would have been chary of using to an author of any kind in his publisher's office, 'You have a good reason for publishing a *New Verse* anthology.' He flipped through the manuscript again. 'You have crossed out your own poems.' I explained I had done so from a certain modesty, a certain squeamishness that had to do with Riding and Graves and their condemnation of anthologies. 'Nonsense,' said Eliot again. 'Nonsense,' or whatever word he used. 'Put them back.' I don't say he praised the poems, but he induced in the poet some needed self-confidence. Perhaps no one quite realizes how it felt, how wonderful it felt, in one's twenties or thirties, to be, solo, in the presence of that Grand Cham of modern writing, discussing a book more or less of one's own.

Even now, though, more than forty years later, I feel a little uneasy when someone talks of 'Geoffrey Grigson the anthologist', the effect of Riding and Graves not having worn off altogether. It was fuelled now and again with sneers. A none too amiable neighbour, with whom I was having a boundary row, once turned on me and said 'All you do is steal other people's poems and put them into books.' He was someone who wouldn't even have read James Bond or more than the *News of the World*, so he must have picked up that bit of malign information from some colleague in his office.

I should have felt happier over the years had I known that Eliot, though he hadn't cared to make it all that plain to me, actually approved of anthologies. 'To those who like myself take pleasure in anthologies . . . ' began the preface he wrote for an anthology which was published by his own firm.

Why compile anthologies? In hopes that the anthology will make you a penny or two? Yes, though poetry isn't the greatest of money earners. Because there are poems you love, poems you feel everyone should know? That is better. Because some poets haven't been treated as they deserve by posterity? That is best, I think. Include poems by them in your anthology, and some justice comes at last: they are speaking to us at last, we are hearing them at last.

That has been my motive, more and more. A poetic mystery is that some poets somehow manage to write only one, or maybe only two, or three, delightful poems. No publisher is going to publish a modern edition of all of such a poet's rubbish, for the sake of his one poem, but then how are single good poems to go on being read and enjoyed if they are allowed to drop out of anthologies, or if there are no anthologies? Where but in anthologies is a present generation going to discover, let's say, Southey's 'Bishop Hatto,' or Jean Ingelow's 'High Tide on the Coast of Lincolnshire', or Violet Jacob's 'Tam i' the Kirk'?

> *O Jean, my Jean, when the bell ca's the congregation*
> *Owre valley and hill wi' the ding frae its iron mou,*
> *When a body's thochts is set on his ain salvation,*
> *Mine's set on you.*

I have spent hours – I nearly wrote wasted hours – in the Bodleian Library and the British Library searching out the books of verse of the one-, two- or three-poem poets in the hope that they must have written and printed other good poems which have been overlooked. Usually there are no such extra poems. Then there comes some sweet-smelling resurrection. And it is to other men's anthologies – anthologies compiled by poets – that I for one owe knowledge of 'The Churchyard on the Sands' by that poet Lord de Tabley who so mysteriously concealed himself (though he was friendly with Robert Bridges?), and 'The Collier's Wedding' by the clerk of a Newcastle parish, Edward Chicken.

Marvellous, also, to have been able now and again to bring a whole poet, a whole deserving poet, a William Diaper –

Unknown to sex the pregnant oyster swells

– a John Winstanley, out of oblivion. Miserable also if you cannot find a publisher to give him at last the full blessing of print. Marvellous, also, to pass one's gold detector over what one supposed to have been a thoroughly explored body of manuscript and find the instrument reacting, excitedly. It was on an exceedingly bitter day in the winter of 1945 (a day when my overcoat was stolen) that among the mass, the untidy mass it was in those days, of John Clare's manuscripts or transcripts in the Northampton Public Library I came across the poem 'Hesperus,' nearly a hundred years after Clare had written it in his asylum:

> *Hesperus! the day is gone,*
> *Soft falls the silent dew,*
> *A tear is now on many a flower*
> *And heaven lives in you.*
>
> *Hesperus! the evening mild*
> *Falls round us soft and sweet,*
> *'Tis like the breathing of a child*
> *When day and evening meet.*
>
> *Hesperus! the closing flower*
> *Sleeps in the dewy ground,*
> *While dews fall in a silent shower*
> *And heaven breathes around.*

Hesperus! thy twinkling ray
Beams in the blue of heaven,
And tells the traveller on his way
That Earth shall be forgiven!

That was worth the stolen overcoat, coming across such an unknown poem, and having the chance to recognize its profundity, and set it in that strong flow of pure sentiment which is our literature, the good essence of our being through centuries of our history and our language.

Taking home in my briefcase this poem no one knew, no one, I thought, had had the chance of knowing (though I discovered afterwards that it had once been printed – and buried – in a local paper soon after Clare had written it) rewarded life, and curiosity about its values.

I cannot conceive that a time will come when all these as yet unknown or unrecognized stores have been exhausted, when anthologizing and exploration have no further point or use. One day some courageous explorer, some persistent anthologizer, will have to pick his way through the lyrics of all our pop songs, over deserts of milkless milk and silkless silk, in search of what can be found even there, in the interests of man.

Though not so rewarding, it will be like going through all the Elizabethan song books.

24 – EDITORS

The first literary editor into whose company and whose office I intruded, briefly, was J. C. Squire. I was upstairs, downstairs and out on the Fleet Street pavement in ten minutes, feeling distinctly glum. We didn't attract one another, and I think I must have asked this bored and rather dull seeming character, this editor-plus-literary editor about the possibility of finding a job on a paper rather than a specialized job on a literary magazine like his own. Squire said 'Are you interested in politics?' I said I wasn't interested in politics. Squire said 'Oh, well . . . ' and that was that, in a book-stuffed scene I pictured with rather more detail in that early autobiography which I called *The Crest on the Silver*. When, soon after, I found a humdrum job – but a job – in Fleet Street itself, in the London Office of the *Yorkshire Post*, I was at least and at last given an occasional book to review, in the boring run of semi-political reporting.

The *Yorkshire Post* had no real literary editor, and the next, the second, of the kind I encountered was a literary editor even more distinctly in decay than drunken Squire (whom his friends of the 'Squirearchy,' as his enemies called them, tried to save by encouraging or persuading authority to give him a knighthood).

This second literary editor looked after the book pages of the *Morning Post*. He had a large stomach, he wore a soft hat of the kind known in those days to such as himself as a cunt-hat. Having read classics, at Balliol I think, he would try now and then to insert some indecent message into the Personal Column, disguised in Greek lettering – *Ει ἄμ ἀφύκκιη ῥαμ* escaped the sub-editors one night. I succeeded him on the *Morning Post*, having been employed first of all to do the work he was too decayed and too lazy to do. His old colleagues didn't like to sack him, to their credit, so they saved his face, and there was I, a literary editor in his twenties, commissioning Christmas articles from Walter de la Mare (a sharp businessman, I recall) or reviews of fiction from a rather silent and aloof David Garnett, famous then for his *Lady into Fox*.

Did I ever know a virtuous literary editor? Did I ever know one with an unfaltering conscience, a literary editor, a single literary editor, not given to compromise or betrayal? One. Joe Ackerley of *The Listener*, whom some of his elder colleagues in the BBC did their best now and again, to get rid of, in part, I imagine, because they knew him to be homosexual. On one occasion this honest and subtle writer and man of letters was saved only by E. M. Forster's direct intervention with the Director-General of the Corporation. Of course Forster himself was known to be homosexual, but his fame and genius made him immune, and more than a little moral influence in literary affairs was accorded to him, as in the matter I recall later of Roy Campbell's knobkerrie attack on Stephen Spender, when Campbell was a talks producer employed by the BBC. This time Forster complained to the Director-General that a servant of such genius could be ill-spared.

Of course, Joe Ackerley knew that this book or that book had to be reviewed, but one thing which distinguished his editorship was matching the book and the reviewer. Who would say honestly what he thought, pro or con? Who could say it well, with skill himself in the writing? Who had a sense, including an historical sense of literature and literary relationship – supposing that wit and taste and value were involved? If Joe was prejudiced, his prejudice was against the shoddy, the shoddy book or a shoddiness in his reviewer's account of it. If he was gentle, he was also unrelenting. If in some ways or to some degree he lived the often sad life of a lonely homosexual in days when you had to be on public and private guard in your homosexuality, what mattered to Joe was quality, irrespective of the sexual keeping of author or contributor. And he was unrelentingly curious. Literature wasn't everything. His book pages had to cover a width of interest. The BBC talks he chose for publication had in the same way to match diversity of interest and concern. Little or nothing he found alien, this cultured man doing a journalist's job.

25 – GEORGE BARNES

Perhaps editor was the right term for George Barnes as Director of Talks in the BBC, and I look back to him as a far better editor than those of us who were his producers were always ready to allow.

It was a tricky job which he held down. Above all it was drummed into producers that the BBC was a monopoly, and that monopolists were always in danger. 'Don't go too far,' 'Don't allow your offerings to stray too far from the acceptable mean,' 'There are interests which mustn't be offended.'

This could have comic effects. I was due one Sunday to repeat from London a talk which had gone out first on the West Regional programme. The Director of Talks, George Barnes's predecessor Sir Richard McConnochie, a safe man who had served his country, before retirement, as British Minister in Afghanistan, took charge to allow his producers a night off. The rehearsal proceeded. The talk was about Gainsborough, and when I came to a paragraph telling that chestnut of a story about Gainsborough throwing his brush down as he painted Mrs Siddons and saying in exasperation 'Damn it, Madam, your nose is too long,' Sir Richard pressed the talk-back key, and there came to me in the studio the voice of the Director of Talks saying 'You know it's a rule that the word *damn* isn't broadcast on a Sunday. I think we must clear that *damn* of yours, Grigson, with the Director of Religious Broadcasting.'

I said, 'Well, it was Gainsborough's *damn*, not mine.'

'Quite so, Grigson, but we had better clear it,' and from behind his glass he had a brief phone conversation with religious authority, religious propriety and fear of offence, pressed the key down again, and announced 'We can go ahead. It's OK.'

He didn't appear to find the occasion at all risible.

George Barnes in his tenure of Talks Department was still cautious; if not as cautious as all that, cautious enough to earn from us

rather an unfair nickname. We called him the Pillar of Marshmallow, tough enough as he was in completing and pushing through his
plans for the famous, too short-lived Third Programme of which he
became Director (he fancied Basil Taylor, by the way, as a future
Director of the Third Programme. But it would never have done.
Basil was no compromiser, and would have sensed – and rejected –
compromise all along the line.)

When he had become Sir George, in season, and one of the
loftiest grandees of broadcasting and the boss of television, he was
involved once in an apple orchard event which shows how well this
son of an Indian KCSI, and graduate of King's, Cambridge, this
compromising yet virtuous Pillar of Marshmallow, was trained in
governmental or ruling class propriety, and considering or attempting always the right thing, without beastliness or cruelty or such a
proceeding as instant or slow dismissal. A young television producer
attached to one of the Regional Centres which looked after
broadcasting outside London, ran off with a girl who was married.
That in itself was nothing to worry either the local or metropolitan
authorities of broadcasting, who did not interfere with the private life
of the staff. But this was different. Private threatened to become
public. The girl, of startling beauty, with a well-known father, was
married to a Member of Parliament in the Region. Mightn't the
newspapers, national as well as regional, find and exploit a
scandal ... headlines ... sensation ... BBC producer cited, the
Divorce Courts ... ?

There was much telephoning, much anxious discussion between
the Regional Director and London, i.e. George Barnes. What
should be done? The producer lived – or his also celebrated parent,
lived in Kent, not far from the Barnes household; and coming home
one weekend his mother announced that George's wife had been on
the phone inviting him to supper. He was mystified: he wasn't
socially intimate with the Great Man. He changed, drove the short
distance to the Barnes household, and was greeted at the door by
George's wife, by Lady Barnes, whom he had never met, with the
news that George was still in the orchard, picking apples.

'Come and give me a hand,' said George, from up a tree, where he was perched in the late sunshine of a cloudless autumn day.

'There's another basket there,' said George, calling him by his Christian name, which he had never done before.

'Coxes,' said George, 'A lovely crop.' The TV producer climbed the ladder and balanced the basket in a fork.

'Four beauties there,' said George. 'Can you reach them?'

'Just,' said the producer.

'Are you happy in your work,' said George, addressing his subordinate once more by his Christian name.

'Perfectly,' said the producer, seeing a glimmer of light. 'Perfectly.'

'If your basket's full,' said George, 'there's another one down there at the back of the tree.'

'Good,' said George when he climbed up the ladder again. 'Try a new branch. Ever thought of joining this new commercial television?'

'No.'

'There must be some good jobs going there,' said George.

'There must be,' said the errant producer.

'Well, it's about supper time.' And so that sunny interview among the fading and falling apple leaves and the pattering Cox's Orange Pippins, just the right apple for the occasion, came to an end. The tableau had been perfect. No more was said. Not a word about running off with an MP's young and beautiful wife.

The supper was good, the conversation affable and inconsequent. The simple upshot – whatever may have been entered on his file –was that the producer was promoted sideways, just a little, out of danger's way. (The truth, or authority's real estimate on a file of one kind or another sometimes came to the subject's knowledge by accident or oversight. A colleague of mine who had delivered many talks for the Corporation, joined the staff, looked up himself in a speaker's file, and found on his card which had not been removed, 'speaks quite well, but far too pushing'.) This was Frank Gillard.

Years later, after George had left the BBC and become chancellor of the new University of Keele, indeed after his death, Programme Four, in the new order of things in broadcasting, celebrated George and his invention and conduct of the Third Programme, and asked me to contribute a memorial poem – if the adjective does not sound too gloomy. Here it is printed, in fact reprinted in the thought and hope that George mightn't have been displeased by it:

Remembering George Barnes, who started the Third Programme

> *Not given to Scotch eggs and shandy in the pub,*
> *But crushing your popadams in the Oriental Club,*
> *Or pacing between BH and Harley Street,*
> *Upset, dear George, but seldom indiscreet,*
> *You showed yourself, whatever you were at,*
> *Never the uncultivated culture-democrat.*
> *You would have preferred pursuing knowledge,*
> *Provost of the best-lawned Cambridge college –*
> *A cynic? No. Perhaps a compromiser,*
> *By nurture, between the average and the wiser.*
> *For which we had the lip to call you shallow,*
> *And nicknamed you the Pillar of Marshmallow,*
> *But then you saw a condition of the mind to come*
> *Pillared on caryatids of nastier chewing-gum,*
> *And salved your admitted treason to the Word*
> *With that great programme so quickly given the bird.*
> *Ear-counting colleagues jeered at Barnes's Folly*
> *And your ridiculous elitist squandering of lolly*
> *Better dispensed to purchase nastier names*
> *And set up series of more babyish parlour games.*
> *'George will hire the Greek Ambassador to read, in Greek,*
> *All Aeschylus, in 99 instalments, week by week.'*
> *Yet for a while, pursued by the easy sneer,*
> *Great words, great notes waved through the startled air,*
> *For a while the bay-trees in the black tubs glistened,*
> *And even the Muses sent for a radio, and listened.*

As normality – of a kind – returned with the end of the war nothing worried George Barnes so much as the thought that persons of a new type might gradually take over the control of broadcasting and change its ideal – his ideal – of broadcasting as an elevating service. Temporary war-time staff might have to be confirmed in office. George, earnest student of Trollope's novels, whose most admired kind of man was the naval officer (he had gone up to Cambridge, to King's, from the Royal Naval College at Dartmouth, disappointed and grieved to have been rejected on the grounds of health) was clear in his mind about the educated and social governance of broadcasting. The kind of young man who in season would be chosen for her Cabinet by Mrs Thatcher would have cut little ice with him if they had looked for a job in the BBC – *his* BBC. So here is a last true tale about him. He didn't fancy the establishment of a Controller instead of a Director of Television. The Director was Norman Collins the novelist, who thought – George thinking otherwise – that he should naturally be upgraded into the new post of Controller, without having to compete, without the post being advertised, and without the candidate being approved by an Appointments Board.

His style wasn't one George cared for. He didn't like the title or ethos of Norman Collins's novel *London Belongs to Me*, he didn't fancy the BBC or rather television belonging to Norman Collins; and he was able to insist that the post should be advertised, leaving Collins to apply for it in the usual way.

Having pulled this off – and caused much ill-feeling – he found himself going home to Kent one afternoon by train. He was tired. He settled down in his corner to catch up with his reading of *The Times*, behind which he fell asleep. It wasn't a corridor train, and at one stop another passenger entered the carriage, and settled down in the corner opposite George, and buried himself behind the *Evening Standard*.

George woke up and put his paper down. The other occupant at that moment put down his *Evening Standard*; and George found himself face to face with the man whose advancement he had at any rate hindered, out of his care for the future conduct of television: Norman Collins.

They had some way to go. Who spoke first? What did they say to each other? Or did they regard each other in silence?

George never told me that. But he was well enough trained, I am sure, to carry matters off with the requisite Whitehall aplomb and good manners, and to show quite the minimum of visible embarrassment.

26 – DARTINGTON HALL

After the war there was no possibility of re-establishing or re-assembling that Hampstead we had shared. Ben Nicholson and Barbara Hepworth were fixed in Cornwall. Henry Moore had given up London altogether for his base in Hertfordshire. MacNeice had moved to the centre of London, Auden was never likely to come back from America, where the grander German and Central Europeans had found themselves more genially and profitably welcomed. In England they were not appreciated, or so they felt. They did not all of them speak very good English, for one thing, witness the jest of Moholy-Nagy's thanks to one of his eminent college hosts in Cambridge. 'Dank you,' he said, shaking hands as the taxi waited to take him to the station on Monday morning, 'for all your hostility.' It was as if an accidental truth lurked in his mispronunciation. Outside the arts and architecture, what academics knew or cared about the Bauhaus?

New Verse, which I had brought to an end at the beginning of the war, before the war turned to bombs and action, was becoming a memory, even though it remained a fairly strong memory. Deciding that neither London in general nor Hampstead in particular was any place for me, and not feeling that the service of the BBC was perfect freedom or perfect servitude, I gave up living at Keynsham which had been our home town at the end of my time with the BBC, and instead of going back to London (our Hampstead home had been damaged, though not destroyed) I looked for a house in Wiltshire, and found one, a farmhouse near the cottage which on and off had been so convenient and so isolated a shelter, tucked away under a chalk escarpment (which was famous among entomologists, I discovered, for its butterflies).

After so large a bite out of our lives the time was now come for some attempted consolidation, freelance, each and all of us under our own power. Some of us had children to be attended to; which added to the fragmentation of our old order in Hampstead.

Ben Nicholson's children – his triplets – began to be schooled now at Dartington Hall; where I wanted my own three to be treated in the warm and sensible ways entirely alien to everything I had experienced at a public gentility school. Once at a parent's meeting or parent-cum-staff meeting at Dartington I met a young headmaster of a mild grammar school, whom I hadn't seen since my own last school year when he joined the staff under my school's ogre of a head, and I asked him why he had chosen Dartington for his own young. He was more liberal in mind than I had guessed. 'Because here,' he replied, 'Everything is opposite to that appalling headmaster's practice and values,' that headmaster of mine having been a lout of a clerical flogger, seldom out of his MA robes (did he sleep in them?), christened Edmund Audley after a Tudor bishop of Salisbury, who was once chancellor of the Order of the Garter. Other distinctions he had none, this brute, except for a love of divided and subdivided school rules, which he and his staff safeguarded with the cane.

In every way his opposite was W. B. Curry, founder and headmaster of Dartington, target for those English controlling existence who approved of flogging because they had been flogged. He was small, lacking in pomposity, a reformer never properly paid for making the lives of children in and out of his own school, and of schools at large, happy instead of miserable. I loved to see him weaving through the children who crowded the quadrangle, smiling at them and joking with them, and being joked with in turn. I liked the way he treated children as more important than parents. (He was succeeded – astonishing error – by a joint headmastership, by two married heads whom the children quickly christened Hugh and Spew. When Hugh and Spew together, or Hugh and Spew severally, walked through the quadrangle, they were ignored, without smiles and without jokes.)

I write this, not to score off a headmaster and a headmistress out of keeping, out of tone, with the exceptional school they were called on to control, but because of the way Curry was publicly treated after his death, or because of the way he wasn't treated at all. *The Times*, for instance, gave this pioneer no obituary, which with a vengeance was fitting him to a backwardness in our age.

We run our prejudices hard at times. And this silence about one of the greatest of modern educators and headmasters and humanizers was restoring or continuing a familiar status quo. It was restoring an old self-satisfaction, and such sneers were infectious and increased.

What did Curry's successors, I have often asked myself, think of the existence so well placed on the school grounds, overlooking the grass slopes of Devonshire and among the pines, of a reclining figure in Hornton stone by Henry Moore?

How much would so many more say 'We told you so,' when this pioneer school began, I suppose inevitably, to show symptoms of change, and decay?

There are some items of literary fact – literary gossip if you like, but gossip is spice for all except saints and misanthropes, unless it is obviously untrue and palpably out of keeping – so bizarre as to light up a small lamp in the memory which is never extinguished. I heard one evening in the gilded ornate library of a French *château*, from a member of her family, that Rebecca West was seduced – that's an old-fashioned word for you – by H. G. Wells in a hansom cab. It perhaps needs explaining to younger readers, who may or may not have seen a hansom cab, in a museum, that this would have been an awkward, if not athletic or contortionist job, a hansom, with its driver overhead, having been a tall narrow vehicle with little room except for two side by side in a normal position. Still, H. G. Wells wasn't a very large man.

In the same *château*, in the salon, the owner pointed to the fire-basket and said 'Packets of letters from Proust were burnt there' – letters in gold ink on purple paper, or was it the other way round, purple ink on gold paper? – because they insulted his great-grandmother who was of Parsee descent.

———

Another item of odd fact – or gossip, but no, I heard it from the man concerned, my friend David Higham, the literary agent. He acted for the once successful but not in fact very talented novelist Francis Brett Young. Some time before Brett Young's death in 1954, David visited the Youngs in their rather ugly bracken encircled holiday house on the hill side above Talland Bay in Cornwall, and remarked one day on the nice woollen socks he was wearing. 'I knitted them,' his wife Jessica said, 'and I will knit you a pair.'

David awaited the socks after a suitable knitting interval, but they never came. Some time after Brett Young's death a limp parcel arrived at David's office, not long after royalty statements and cheque had been dispatched. Inside was a pair of socks, not darned (and not, I think, washed), with a note from Brett Young's widow saying 'I wasn't able to knit you a pair of socks like the ones you so admired on Francis, so having come across them in a chest of drawers I send you the actual pair.'

David remarked that it was the queerest gift that ever came to him from or in memory of a client.

━━━━━

Forty-five years ago a young Austrian sat on a balcony in Hampstead, in Well Walk, having a late breakfast on her first morning in England. She heard a curious evidently human chanting from the neighbouring balcony, tip-toed over and peered through the creeper. A thin man with a white beard was reading from a manuscript book, and her hostess explained later that he was a poet named Sturge Moore, who was not infrequently to be heard chanting or reading to himself like that.

So much the worse for me. When I and that girl were married she invented a word, to *sturge*. 'Sturging,' she would say to me, 'sturging,' when I went on, too long, reading poems to myself.

━━━━━

We heard a story of Sturge Moore not long after that, when we were staying at the Devil's Bridge, in Wales. It ought to be true, because our informant was a friend of Yeats's, who was a friend of Sturge Moore's, and he said that he and Yeats were present in a barn where they were performing one of Sturge Moore's Greek dramas. The curtain creaked back across the timbers and there advanced white-bearded Sturge Moore in white robes, hieratically chanting his own lines, whereon the voice of Robbie Ross was heard saying too loudly from the back of the barn, 'Here comes the sheep in sheep's clothing.'

Robbie Ross was the witty friend of Oscar Wilde, and, as I say, the story fits, though I have heard it told of others than Sturge Moore, and Ross, and of other events than sturging in that barn, which was on the Cotswolds, I have forgotten to add.

———

Scene: a party in Bloomsbury, given by Naomi Mitchison.
Guests: among them Wystan Auden, Christopher Isherwood, Henry Green the novelist (whom I found disappointingly dull to talk to) and Naomi Mitchison's remarkable brother, J. B. S. Haldane, who inclined to be as ominously silent as Naomi Mitchison was voluble. Also myself sitting a little disconsolately on or in a deep sofa; on which suddenly, Naomi Mitchison flops, dressed in an ancient Athenian manner in a robe held in by wide ribbons. She is out of breath. Silence. Then in a husky voice, she says 'It's all very difficult. What *is* poetry?'
Silence from me as well.

———

Naomi Mitchison, let it be remembered, wrote (in the *New Statesman*) the first civil and perceptive review of anything written by a young poet named Auden.

———

There are remarks, events, approaches which leave us at once embarrassed beyond hope of escape or quick enough recovery. I think it was at that same party given by Naomi Mitchison that I was all of a sudden confronted by Margaret Gardner, daughter of Percy Gardner, the Oxford professor who wrote so confidently about the master works of Greek sculpture which no longer exist. Perhaps it was that intellectual parentage which so inclined her to be the friend (and patron too) of modernity in one form or another.

Confronting me, she said 'Geoffrey, why don't you like me?'

How did I get out of that one? In a cowardly denial, I expect. But I do remember how I confusedly tried to recover balance on another occasion. Michael Ayrton, son of the novelist and reviewer Gerald Gould whom Wyndham Lewis once referred to as a 'certain G. G. or hack' (but no man can be held to blame for the shortcomings of his father or mother), dragged me into his studio near Broadcasting House to look at his pictures, which I detested. I was expected to comment on the latest of them. I could think of nothing to say except about two cats which were playing round the foot of an easel. 'How nice to have two cats instead of one,' I said.

———

'I've been to see Sturge Moore,' said Andrew Young who had come to have a cup of tea in Keats Grove. 'I told him that I was read by the young, and he wasn't.' Andrew was far from the most talkative of poets, and he left without saying much else.

Some of the slightly less young had never bothered to notice that Andrew's poems existed, but this aloof cleric (Presbyterian minister, then Church of England parson) didn't much care, I supposed. An old friend from his Edinburgh youth, who managed Bumpus's Bookshop in Oxford Street, published them in small inexpensive editions which made no splash, and for him that had been enough.

When praise and selected and collected editions came in his old age, I suspect he would have welcomed more understanding of the poet he was. Like some other poets who expressed themselves through unfashionable 'nature' (Edward Thomas for one) he found himself in wrong hands, to some degree. But he wasn't going to object. His poems were his own business, though you could be allowed to share them.

———

A letter once came to me from Cecil Day Lewis, whom I very seldom met, and whose poems I came to dislike, with reason I think, in which he said 'I shall give Wystan Auden a run for his money.'

———

In fact I think I met Day Lewis only once, in the strict neutrality of a studio in Broadcasting House, where he read the poems by Crabbe I had chosen for a programme. So I can say there was nothing personal in the feud – see the life of Day Lewis written by his son – I was supposed to maintain with him.

Edith Sitwell I never met, though when I was an undergraduate I once saw her on a platform. And listened to her (introduced to the undergraduate audience by Tom Driberg, of Christ Church).

Listening to her was enough.

———

I had been with Wyndham Lewis to a Bond Street exhibition of Rowlandson – Lewis greatly admired Rowlandson, not surprisingly – and I wanted him to come with me to another exhibition, a few doors away, at Tooth's Gallery, where the floor manager, so to say, was a suave, over-smart young man, given to dealer's snootiness, named Keene. 'No,' said Lewis, 'no, thy Tooth is far too Keene.'

Lewis wasn't given to repeating himself, so I don't think it was a *mot* he had had occasion to make before or ever made again.

———

It is unwise to leave some 'do' or reception in a fog, talking too loudly when you can't see who is ahead of you or behind you.

Clive Bell, the 'scarecrow of an advanced fool-farm' in Wyndham Lewis's novel *Tarr*, was taking a foggy way along the pavement from a reception given by the Duchess of Westminster. He was twirling a stick and saying, or chanting to himself as though it were a song,

'Good night, Duchess, Duchess.
Good night, Duchess.'

Unaware that behind him and unseen by him in the fog was Osbert Sitwell, who saw to it that the story was quickly around London.

———

'Talk to me, Miss West. Don't talk to my husband. He is uneducated, and common' – Emma Hardy to Rebecca West, taking tea with the Hardys at Max Gate.

When I was at Dorchester looking for information about William Barnes, an elderly Dorchester shopkeeper described to me how Thomas Hardy used to come into the back of the shop and complain about the way Emma Hardy nagged him.

———

Rather desolate fields without or with only a few paths or tracks stretched away from the farm-house I bought in Wiltshire at the end of the war. Curlew flighted from an escarpment to these damp fields, the damp meadows of long coarse grass, saying *curlu, curlu*, as if it were Yorkshire and not Wiltshire.

Edward Thomas knew these fields intimately and used to cross them from his uncle's home in Swindon to meals with an old lawyer in Wootton Bassett, a dismal little town in those days which matched the fields. When this lawyer was suspected of prostate trouble, the Wootton Bassett doctor demanded a specimen of his water.

'You must have it? Really?'

'Yes, Willie, a bottleful.'

'A large bottle?'

'No, Willie; a medium bottle, I will send one down.'

Days went by and then this Willie Gough's clerk arrived at the doctor's with a parcel done up in pink legal tape, sealing-waxed. Layer by layer was peeled away. More paper, more tape, more sealing-wax, revealing an old pair of soft bedroom slippers, tucked into each other. There at last, between the slippers, was the required bottleful.

This Willie Gough greatly valued his friendship with Edward Thomas, and wanted me to come over and read letters Thomas had written him, and manuscripts. Foolishly I never did. Lawyer Gough died and all his papers were burnt in a huge bonfire in his garden.

The farmer who rented the tumbledown farm buildings and stack yard which had once gone with the house I bought, knew Edward Thomas and taught him to make hay ropes.

The last farmer who lived in the house and his sister with him had their own peculiar history. The sister had a child by a solicitor's clerk away in London, and then she had two more children by her brother. The two incestuous children were boarded out not far away. Then in time the brother died, followed soon after by the sister. In her will nothing was left to the two, by that time grown-up children. Everything went to the child by the solicitor's clerk – a case, between illegitimacy and incest, of comparative respectability.

That was real, if not Georgian or essay writers' North Wiltshire in the forties, in a country which was still inhabited, as Wiltshire's John Aubrey had written soon after the Civil War, by aborigines inclined to be phlegmatic and slow and heavy of spirits and feggy.

———

Willie Gough's specimen packed between bedroom slippers reminds me that just down from his house a pair of bedroom slippers was the price I once paid for a fifteenth-century Virgin and Child which I had often noticed hidden away among flowers in the front garden of a cottage. One day when I was feeling a little sorry for myself, I thought 'I'll buy that statue.' I knocked at the door, and the nearly bald old lady who answered, said yes, I could have it if I bought her a new pair of bedroom slippers; which I did. An odd price for a medieval work of art.

———

A quotation many of us favoured was from Wyndham Lewis's *One Way Song*, about Eliot, though we were loyal to him and had respected him so as deliverer and great enlivener:

> *I seem to note a roman profile bland*
> *I hear the drone from out the cactus-land:*
> *That must be the poet of the Hollow Men:*
> *The lips seem bursting with a deep Amen.*

Wasn't it too late – but then there came Auden's rather peculiar Christianity – for light or deep Amens?

———

I never heard T. S. Eliot laugh.

———

One of Wyndham Lewis's stories was that Clive Bell had been deputed to investigate Eliot, that strange young man from America and from the City, who wrote such novel poems and such magisterial (if still in those days anonymous) essays and *de novo* estimates in *The Times Literary Supplement*.

Clive Bell reported that he spoke with scarcely a trace of *American accent*.

J. C. Squire, though, considered it safe to remark in his *London Mercury* about Eliot's *Waste Land* that 'a grunt would serve equally well.' It was a judgement he paid for.

———

It was a long, long time before I ever visited Rupert Brooke's Grantchester, and when I was persuaded to go there at last, what did I find but a pub named after him. The only pub named after an English poet – except, no doubt, those special cases of Byron or Shakespeare?

I was prejudiced. I grew up *not* to admire Rupert Brooke. I grew up – eventually – as one of Auden's party:

> *For gasworks and dried tubers I forsook*
> *The clock of Grantchester, the English rook,*

and though I keep a softness for the glitter and the cawing of the English rook, no doubt I could learn much of myself were I to analyze why exactly I've never been able to read Brooke's competent poems with any relish. Self-satisfaction – I mean Brooke's apparent satisfaction with Brooke? The glorification of Brooke after his early death at a right moment for his special fame, via the wrong eulogists? Or do I discover the answer in what I have already quoted from a letter written about him by E. M. Forster, describing Brooke's charm and also his essential hardness?

I think I would say about him, as an item in this book so far as it amounts to a memoir of *me*, what I have also felt about the poems, and more, of my coeval Cecil Day Lewis.

———

When was the word 'homintern' invented? I won't say that in the late thirties it was intellectually fashionable or acceptable to denigrate a writer or a painter because he was homosexual, though the fact might be mentioned in conversation if he was a bad writer or a bad painter, and aggressive, and conceited, and in a position to promote other bad writers, or bad painters, for homosexuality's sake.

I do have to admit that round about the time of the Surrealist Exhibition several of us did feel that a conspiracy of homosexuals needed a curb. The possible nature of such a curb was discussed. One plan was to print inside a box – in *New Verse* or the *Surrealist Bulletin* or elsewhere – the names of these aggressive homosexual excluders in alphabetical order, with no comment, no heading at all. Everyone would guess why the names were rounded up like that, and if the name of someone who wasn't 'queer' was accidentally included, there could be no danger of a libel action.

Neat, but it never came off. Paul Nash was among those who favoured and discussed the plan and I think the discussion took place, only to be rejected, in Herbert Read's Hampstead studio.

———

When Wyndham Lewis came home from his wartime sojourn in America and Canada he remarked that it had been enjoyable to feel for a while without roots. That surprised me, until I began to think about it, to think about the danger to writer and artist of becoming pot-bound, the hard sides of the pot pressing against you, and your roots using up the nutrients in the soil, define soil and nutrient as you may.

Why did Auden go to America? Because a war was coming? Why not, if he realized strongly enough that he had one life, one talent, one duty, to his talent. Frederick Prokosch says in his *Voices: A Memoir* that he asked Auden why he decided 'to escape to America'. Auden replied that his coming to America hadn't been an escape, it hadn't even been a decision: it had been an instinct, a desire.

An extra early premonition, too, of becoming pot-bound?

28 – JOHN PIPER

Do we ask why we fall in love? 'Fall' in the usual circumstances isn't so bad a term. We 'fall', that is to say, a sudden fall or a slow fall. Suddenly or slowly we discover how we fit the circumstances and the companionship we find ourselves in. We accept and we don't question, though we may, and should question our falling out of love, if it occurs: we worry at finding and analyzing the reasons, if we have courage and persistence enough; and then, too, we may at last begin to understand why it was the love began.

This has been so in my relationship with – I was going to say the artist, but I shall say the man, John Piper, who will have no need to be embarrassed in any way by an ambiguity in the word 'love'. Our relationship began in the early Thirties, and seemed to dwindle and fade some ten years later. It was a momentous time for me, when I had settled with a job in Fleet Street and married and when I came to know Henry Moore and Ben Nicholson, and Wyndham Lewis, and Auden, and had started *New Verse*. It was Henry Moore who told me I should like John Piper (still at that time a solicitor in the London County Council) and that there was much to be said for his pictures, which I had been complaining were rather sketchy or slight (the picture I had in the sight of mind was one longer than tall, in which gulls – white gulls – were wavering to and fro. I was judging it from a pale reproduction in the *Bookman*, which wasn't fair).

In my own family, among my brothers, scattered and some of them dead by that time, life and appetite were ruled by a strong feeling for place and the past, going back, at least as far as people and ancestors were concerned, to a grandfather (I never knew him) who helped to run the Norfolk and Norwich Archæological Society, found Roman horse-harness, or bridle-pieces rather, in his pond, liked 'to know where he was with people and relations,' and so knew everything he could know about the pedigrees of his county. The taste wasn't so strong in my father, living more or less in unfamiliar exile in Cornwall, but it crossed a bridge of space and time and was embodied for me in one of my six brothers in particular, a brother older than I was by seven years, a mathematician, a musician, and a classical scholar.

In spite of our difference in age we explored together (the range of local exploration wasn't very wide in those bicycle days, but the exploration was intense), we shared fun and values together, I learnt from him in one sphere of sensation and of interest; and then I lost him, in the vicious trench warfare of Flanders. He was just, I suppose, blown to pieces.

That loss, I was to realize slowly, left an extraordinary blank which I never filled. And then I came to know John Piper, and to find myself, for a while, peacefully living again in a second family of two.

What were we both like? A then and a now were presented to us, I think I can say, in unison. What were the things we liked? They were, or they included, barrows, standing stones, churches, ruins, outcrops of rock, limestone especially, caves, waterfalls, etchings and water-colours by Cotman, full moonlights by Samuel Palmer.

Flowers were not much in John's line, which was a pity – wild flowers, I mean, rarities and treasures scattered across England and Wales. But we liked impossible jokes, catch-phrases, verbal nonsense of every kind, guidebooks, at least the Victorian ones by parsons and scholars and antiquaries, which had something to say, and guided us to much that seemed forgotten or disregarded, especially those detailed red guidebooks which had been published by John Murray. We liked picnics too; and listing it here out of place, we had a very special liking for William Blake – 'Mr Blake's skin don't dirt.' Also with a slight mockery, if that isn't too strong a word, we liked singing hymns ancient and modern (a favourite was 'O that I had wings of angels') with John at his piano. Mine was the slight mockery of the parson's son, it wasn't nostalgia for evensong by oil-lamp, and the lost vicarage existence.

In some items on that list I am wrong to say *we*. John would certainly have added much more, which was outside my range. But for me John Piper was what that lost brother would have been, in full, unquestionably, if now and then in a different guise.

And so I come to the word, the name, the place-name, Bell Busk. There we alighted.

'*Bell Busk Station*' – I am quoting, and we had it with us, from Murray's *Handbook for Travellers in Yorkshire and for Residents in the County. Third Edition; thoroughly revised*, my copy having belonged to the famous Victorian geologist and explorer of limestones in Devonshire and of Kent's Cavern, William Pengelly –

'*is the nearest to Malham (5m.) – close to which are Gordale and Malham Cove, two of the most remarkable scenes in Great Britain . . . Hence the visitor should walk to Gordale Scar and the 'Cove', a round of between 2 and 3 m. Gordale should first be visited (Gordale = the narrow valley?) (Gore = a slip). The stream which descends through it, E. of the village, will be a sufficient guide. The approach is between two ranges of limestone cliffs; which offer nothing particularly noticeable until, on turning a projecting corner of rock, you find yourself in front of the 'chasm' as it is sometimes called. The impression is one of absolute awe, especially if the place to be visited alone, and toward evening.*

> '*Gordale chasm, terrific as the air*
> *Where the young lions couch,*'

writes Wordsworth, who was always 'full of praises for the fine scenery of Yorkshire'. Gordale Scar, near Malham, he declares to be one of the grandest objects in nature, though of no great size. It has never disappointed him.'

Typical. Wordsworth for both of us, James Ward's huge, in those days rather despised landscape in the Tate Gallery for both of us, rare plants at Malham Cove and round about for me, a monstrous gateway to a super-romantic, out of fashion, stony paradise of caves and scars and waterfalls – waterfalls which John proceeded, as we trudged from one to another, to draw in ink and water-colour.

Not far away were the mountains of Ingleborough and Whernside, and various pot-holes in which tree tops appeared more or less level with the rough, surrounding limestone surfaces, giant arum lilies of limestone. Scenes too were nearby by which Turner as well as James Ward had painted, the two of them trudging round – we were not so hardy – until the skin was off their feet.

Understand limestone and cave and cliff, pictures and poems and presences of the Romantic times now revived, and you understand, whatever was to be built on it, a foundation of Piper's art. And how much more there was to follow, to be sketched, and to be made the basis of what have been called since pictures of Piper's Places – places in other counties which few seemed to value or know at that time, in mid-Devon, South Devon, North Devon, in Wiltshire, in Wales, in the Vale of Neath, where streams tumbled over hard ledges curving outward so that you could shelter behind them, or went rumbling down hill into darkness. And it wasn't, though enemies or scorners declared that it was, as if this most versatile of artists, as he was to show himself, was deserting modernity for sentimentalities of the past. He was creating a theatre, a proscenium of English past and European present. Then in his flint farmhouse outside Henley, in a dry valley beyond the mile of trees planted by Gainsborough's brother, what extraordinary hospitality John Piper and his wife Myfanwy displayed.

In 1939 John Piper and I passed the last night before the declaration of war in my cottage in Wiltshire. We had passed through Wroughton in the evening. Blackout cloth was being nailed up over the public house windows. People drinking were unusually noisy. That small town or large village seemed unusually hollow and ill at ease. In the morning we drove off to Uffington to have lunch with John Betjeman, stopping on the way and stationing a battery set on the yellow stubbles in time to hear Chamberlain say we were at war.

All three of us were old enough to remember catch phrases from World War One. John Betjeman poured out sherry, and with the Betjeman half-smile said 'For the Duration,' once familiar words from our childhood.

Were bombs going to fall, how soon? How soon would sirens be screaming and all-clears soothing the night?

The Pipers filled their house. Apprehension or no, suppers as pleasant as any I have known were eaten at the long table in front of a wide fire of beech logs, to the light of a battery of candles in white candlesticks. No one quarrelled, nobody disagreed with anyone else – or that seems my impression now.

I am not sure how long that community life continued. There were still expeditions, though petrol became short and cars were shut away in the huge ramshackle barn. There were still jokes by candle-light, or winging their way in on postcards – was it then or later that a postcard came from Tom Kendrick, head of the British Museum (which was busily emptied into the old stone-mines of Corsham) with a crude drawing of an old countryman announcing in crude lettering from his mouth 'Oi traps lomacks,' which derived from the name of the rather fussy old-worldish ecclesiologist and ritualist Trappes-Lomax? Haydn poured still out of John Piper's immensely long-trumpeted gramophone, which gave no sense of being a Last Trump. We watched images forming on the films John Piper developed down in the cellar. More voices sang 'O that I had wings of angels' round the piano.

The legions had scattered somewhat, all the same. No more huge Piperish parties round the house and in the meadow with Hélion and Léger, and Hans Erni among the guests, with Sandy Calder setting his circus of wire animals to perform in a circle of admirers, or taking wire and pliers from his pockets and twisting immediate brooches for his hostess and such girls as caught his eye.

I am not sure that all this agreement wasn't insensibly becoming too agreeable, that all this happiness, which I now find it so difficult to sort out in temporal detail, wasn't staling a little too much.

Perhaps – and I am speaking personally – seeds of a later criticism and disagreement were being invisibly and not altogether consci-ously sown. Perhaps John's rising name helped to fertilize seeds of jealousy?

Were some of us – myself included – quite so ready to believe in the 'modernism' of John's position and his work? And what about some of his friends and some – ah, indeed – some of his patrons? My feeling was that Betjeman, prime friend, prime comedian, was betraying new poetry with old forms, old rhythms and cadences, and playing more than ever to a middle public, complacent and easily pleased. And patrons? Poets and other writers in our world can live, and do live, without patrons. Artists require individuals – rich ones, if possible, who can afford high prices – to buy their individual works. There is no story older than that in the history of art livelihood since the closure of the Middle Ages. Mightn't we think John was showing himself too complacent, too ready to please others, along with himself, in that direction?

Though from years still to come, I shall excerpt two declarations John Piper was to make in his small book about stained-glass:

Declaration A.

'There is one panel of thirteenth-century stained-glass which is very much a part of my life. It is one of the nave windows of the small nave-and-chancel church of Grately in Hampshire. I have known it since I was in my early twenties, when I did a copy of it in water-colours. On the whole I learnt more about using colours when doing this copy than I have ever learned before or since.'

Declaration B.

'What nobody can see today is how to be simple. Only Matisse. He bought up the whole rights of the twentieth century for simplicity!'

Just in which of these statements was John Piper's heart? In both? But why not? Yet it was possible to suspect a preference, a reaction, a return, a rejection, an unwelcome kind of exclusion and coming-clean, a Betjemanism in paint – rather more possible when, for all reasons combined, a withdrawal, my withdrawal, I am afraid, not his, had begun. If the seeds were in fact in the ground, much might be fertilizing them, none too worthily, and working them up into substantial objection.

When I was in Zürich, just after the beginning of peace, I met the Swiss artist Hans Erni again.

'Is John,' he asked, 'altogether given now to castle-romanticism?'

And one thing it takes a long time to learn, one thing I did not learn very well, is the necessity of minding your own business in friendship.

I was staying on that visit to Zürich in a flat where a fellow guest was Benjamin Britten. Did I reflect that Britten and Piper were such friends? Not as I should have done. I was feeling very consciously 'modern', very pro Henry Moore, very pro Ben Nicholson. Staying there too was the film-maker Basil Wright, both of us loathing what we felt as the dull barbarism of Churchill's son-in-law Duncan Sandys, who had helped to spoil a party one night, and to get in the way of my reunion with the Ernis. After the party Basil Wright and I walked up and down the lake shouting Abomination on politicians and uttering loud self-congratulations, in the hearing of the ducks bobbing among the lights across the lake, because *we* had among our friends a genius of modernity whose name, and damn all politicians, was Wystan Auden.

As for jealousies, there were some who did not take kindly to the rather grander patronage by which John was being elevated. Patrons, not, I have to say, not all of them, the most agreeable persons to encounter, tumbled into Fawley Bottom. There was an occasion when the artist Ivon Hitchens, modest and retreative, was staying there for the week-end. Grandees came and went – and then Ivon went, insisting on being taken a day early into the station. He arrived back soon enough in his woodland studio to write and post a letter of indignation or disdain the same evening: 'If you have to behave and entertain like that to be a successful artist . . .', etc., or words of that import, he was glad *not* to be successful.

Kenneth Clark's patronage was commented upon with some scepticism. Oliver Simon the typographer dearly loved both the Pipers and Graham Sutherland and his wife. He felt he had 'discovered' Sutherland's art, he had bought pictures by him, but he couldn't compete with the wealth or influence of Clark and now thought he was being neglected. Which paintings, Piper's or Sutherland's, and which wife did Clark like the more? With some difficulty he managed to get hold of two postcards Clark had written, one to John's wife, one to Sutherland's wife. These he submitted to a friend in the French Embassy whose hobby was deductions from a study of handwriting.

Could a comparison of Clark's hand in these cards reveal a certain preference? Another time Oliver had a chance of listening to Clark's conversation for an evening. Would Clark talk more about Pipers or about Sutherlands? Which wife, Piper's or Sutherland's, would be the more frequently mentioned? Before the Hampstead evening began Oliver filled a trouser pocket with pebbles from his garden path. Every time John's pictures and John's wife were mentioned by Clark, Oliver transferred a pebble to one coat pocket, every time Clark's talk was of Sutherland's pictures and Sutherland's wife a pebble was transferred to the other coat pocket; after which only a count was necessary to settle the preferences and stoke the jealousy.

Childish? But childishness isn't confined to children, and jealousy can be earnest and serious.

Such in part was the climate in which John's reputation was now couched for a while.

29 – JOHN BETJEMAN

Divisive is a word which has fitted the peculiar case of John Betjeman and his poetry, severally, or, together, the two combined. For some he has been something of a pop star of the middle class. How many others have objected, how many have said that this charming jester, in action and in words, in this or that campaign, in public and on television, is in a way æsthetically ridiculous? How many have asked what he really stood for, if he was indeed quite real, and if he was not, on second thoughts, some kind of changeling found under a castor oil plant in the suburbs?

Often the insults have been more insulting, and even bitter and scornful. What were his life's keepings? Wasn't it odd to make verse – skilfully to be sure – into a parody of verse, using forms and metres, even rhythms, adapted from hymn books both to mock those who enjoy them and think them to be the eternal essence of poetry, and to make them enjoy being mocked? 'Culture' without difficulties, 'culture' easily come by, without problems.

The argument, the division does continue. Indignation asks – though now the word 'modern' is out – what have we expected the 'modern' poet to be?

Serious.

Hadn't we taken to Thomas Hardy? Didn't we read the newly discovered Gerard Manley Hopkins, anathema to some, to others the Great Refurbisher (Hardy, too, was a refurbisher in his poems). Didn't we read Hopkins insisting that language had its thew, that to be in earnest was the proper distinction of poets and their writing?

But then fashion was strengthening, and in this acceptance of Betjeman, if many of us, in my generation, continued half cold, or altogether cold, others became more than half warm.

I remember a surge of incredulity, even among admirers of the Betjeman Muse, I would say, when in 1972 Betjeman succeeded that reformed communist Cecil Day Lewis as Poet Laureate. The only parallel I could think of had not been in the small realm of poetry, but years before in the large ragged realm of politics, when several of us in Fleet Street who had tidied up after him and corrected his spelling (and much else) had woken up one morning to find that so tiresome a young man as Anthony Eden, weakly plague of his father-in-law's newspaper, to which he contributed naive political articles and naive articles on current art shows, had been given a first ministerial appointment. Wasn't poetry being sold shorter than ever? And we asked, some of us, what had been whose motive in advising and bringing about an appointment so bizarre?

Perhaps we shall know one day, if it is still of interest, when some hundred years ban on the laureate papers has lapsed.

I say 'so bizarre' because if appointments to this royal office had often been so foolish, the appointments and the poets themselves had always been serious in intention. Poetry has its place for jesters, for light poetry, of course, but who in their day would have thought that Tom Hood or W. S. Gilbert or A. P. Herbert should have been made Poet Laureate?

Was making Betjeman the new Poet Laureate, the new royal representative of this most ancient English art, a pointed joke or a rebuff to 'modernism', deliberately? Or an endeavour – but then Day Lewis, his predecessor in office, had been not merely left but an avowed communist – to exalt a neutral poet when nearly all poets of any ability, or acceptability, were left rather than right?

It did seem the worse in the situation of the time. Hardy and Hopkins – and Eliot too, though without grace – had been more or less absorbed. Auden was writing, and MacNeice. A phase of more lucid, less puzzling 'modernism' was being established. Here was Auden, according to Wyndham Lewis, abounding in speech and destroying that fear of the word, that spell with which Eliot had bewitched many of his close followers and juniors, 'who, after endless painful deliberation, have scribbled half a dozen lines and then fled away for good and all from composition upon such austere terms.' Here we were learning of the existence of Hölderlin in the past and Rilke and Valéry in the present, and were to learn soon of Pasternak and the serious richness of his poetry and his opinions. A book I have conceived that every English poet should read over again once every year is Pasternak's *Letters to his Georgian Friends*, to refresh himself in his view of happiness of life as it should be, 'serious, profound, fathomless and sad, just because of its boundlessness and its magnitude,' and just to re-sharpen and reset his standards.

'One must write wonderful things, make discoveries, and see to it that wonderful things happen to you. That is life. The rest is rubbish.'

'I saw something in life that had some connection with great men . . . I do not say that one ought to hang anyone who is not a genius, but in that case one's approach and one's standards must be quite different.'

Here was Pasternak writing, among his poems of awe and splendour, that very special poem 'The Stars were Racing' in which the grand phenomena of night include the stars, the waves bending around headlands, the Sphinx in the desert listening, the blue shadowed smile of the Sahara at dawn spreading on the lips of the Colossus, the Atlantic breeze from Morocco, daybreak on the Ganges, Archangel snoring in its drifts of snow, and the ink drying – yes – on the draft of Pushkin's great poem 'The Prophet'.

Of course I agreed there can be no Act of Uniformity in verse. Of course I agreed there should be no attempt to impose one. Yet I have been among those never quite able to rid themselves of discomfortable feelings or suspicions about Betjeman's poems, unwilling and certainly unable to swallow him whole, so we had intermittently uneasy contacts, Betjeman and I, through half a century.

Was I blaming him or that increasing Betjemania? Contacts and occasions made me a little ashamed very often.

Was I blaming him for what was none of my business, after all?

Was I so sure that he didn't connive, ever more so, in the Betjemania and its furtherance? At the same time how could anyone help succumbing – well, now and then – to that half-modesty, half-humility, as it seemed?

Like others I was up to the neck in a Betjemanic situation before I quite recognized what was happening, enticed by that personal charm of his, of which he seemed so aware.

I was once rehearsing with Betjeman in a television show at Alexandra Palace, in the days when television went out from those London heights. We had to wait some time for a run-through, and there we were with time on our hands and make-up, the make-up which was necessary in those days, on our faces. 'Let's go and look at the church down there,' said J. B. 'It's a most interesting church' (which it was not, but it was a Victorian or Edwardian church, a cult church). A pair of grease-painted oddities, we found a Corporation car and chauffeur and were driven down the hill. The car waited, and we went through the shabby conifers to examine this pinnacled item of stock brick. We saw a policeman, and the policeman saw us. Betjeman conceived that our made-up faces would excite the policeman's curiosity and suspicion. Were we pansies, and were we also going to rob the offertory box? He was there still when we emerged. He followed us again at a carefully judged distance, out of the churchyard, out of the conifers, at last, on to the pavement. And then of course we reached the car on which the letters BBC were plain, and with the uniformed chauffeur opening the door the two outrageous, shameless, if not actually criminal pansies rolled off up hill to the Palace.

It was funny, yes. It had gone to plan, once the policeman had been spotted. But I felt uneasy and ashamed, just as it must have seemed just a little shaming to some members of an earlier party when Betjeman and his undergraduate friends had filled a motor-coach to go and call on a 'Uranian poet', as bookseller's catalogues would call him now, in his lonely East Anglian parsonage.

Another time I had to pass the night with this amiable jester, this parodist of the modes of *Hymns Ancient and Modern*, in a double bed in the one free room we could find at the Royal Clarence Hotel opposite the cathedral at Exeter, or rather I had to spend the night with Betjeman and his nearly bald Archie, his childhood teddy bear. Embarrassing; or at least I could not summon the right mood for the occasion.

Yet one more occasion. From the next room in a West End art gallery I heard a slow shuffle and a voice I recognized. J. B. came into sight talking with ecstasy, real or assumed, about the canvasses around the walls by Sir Edwin Landseer. I was there – let me excuse myself as one who would sooner have been shuffling round an exhibition of Picasso or Ben Nicholson – in the course of business, having to earn money by writing for some paper or magazine what I thought of a revival of Landseer. John Betjeman seemed to be enjoying a private revel in the wonder of the virtues of Victorian art at nearly its worst, or most treasonable.

Yet a fourth occasion. Exasperated, as I shall explain in writing about Nikolaus Pevsner, by the Great Campaign, æsthetical and then commercial, to re-establish the general credit of Victorian art and architecture (on the whole how much better the Victorians were in literature) I had sent not too heavy but not – so I thought – too unkind or too sarcastic a letter to *The Times* about the way, once more, Betjeman was campaigning to preserve a Victorian building, the demolition of which would hardly damage the culture of England or mankind. Television had lately shown the roof-top of the Marble Arch, and in it a trap-door opening, and out of the trap-door John Betjeman, with his now much publicized bald teddy bear, emerging, and crying, so I pretended, 'Save! Save!'

An exaggeration, and if I did not say it, I felt that when we get rid of a bad building we allow ourselves room and possibility for a good one.

Soon after, Lord Kennet, i.e. Wayland Young, arranged a reception in the House of Lords to mark new regulations which would do more to save buildings under threat. My wife and I were about to climb the stairs, under the gaze of enormous gold-braided footmen, when through the doors from the outer world, from the snow, came John Betjeman. I held out a hand, without a thought of that tiff which – to me – had not seemed monstrous at all. J. B. eyed me with severity, declared he would not shake the hand of someone who could write so detestable a letter to *The Times*, put his hand behind his back, and departed upwards by the lift to the grandeurs of the Royal Gallery and 'The Death of Nelson' and 'The Meeting of Wellington and Blucher'.

Do I believe, as I have been told, that after some earlier pinprick Betjeman climbed from his house at Uffington and cursed me from the backside of the White Horse? Why not? John Betjeman showed himself a kindly and forgiving man; but I detested and still detest his verses, or most of them.

30 — BAD GUY

A danger in writing memoirs is reading into events, into personalities, what you and the world have learnt about them subsequently. So what in fact do I remember about Guy Burgess before he earned the sobriquet of mole, and fled to Russia, and became famous? What do I read back into him? Certainly not that he was fascinating, brilliant, etcetera, and endowed with all the qualities ascribed to him in spy books or mole books by authors who never knew him – and some who did, writers on the sensational make.

For some time during and after the resettlement into peace of a kind I was a colleague. I served, I won't say with, but alongside, and as Burgess would have thought decidedly below him, in the Talks Department of the BBC.

Of 'outstanding intelligence'? Surely not. Average. 'Charming, in mind, in company?' No. Bumptious, to use an old-fashioned word.

Always using the Christian names of the great, the politically great or prominent, the Whitehall people who were talked about and who talked to him, and had done so only that morning or the previous evening. 'Anthony said', 'Winston said.' This wasn't the velvet fur covering the mole: it was his natural covering, no matter what he was up to, his ambivalence.

And then his appearance. He glanced at you with quick rather shifty eyes, to see if you were taking proper notice of the way he was analyzing this or that situation. That look came into his rather puffy face, even if he was sure that you were of no possible importance in his ostensible socio-political scheme of things. The clothes he wore: a correct Whitehall uniform, pin-striped dark trousers, but baggy (the nylon crease hadn't come in, so his trousers looked sloppy, like Brunel's in that famous Victorian photo of Brunel with the chains). His shirt wasn't always clean. When he walked he shambled or shuffled, though quickly, as much as to say 'I have important people to see. Out of the way.'

In his black coat and striped trousers, his uniform which did not fit by a millimetre or two, he looked the homosexual, or the one type of homosexual, that he was.

Producers would go down to the front hall of the BBC to receive the important persons they hoped, or indeed were, to set before the microphone. Producer and speaker might discuss the script; the script on its soft rustle-proof paper required rehearsal, and marking up for emphasis, or throw-away; the script needed timing, lengthening or shortening.

It did not take all that time to form a perhaps somewhat prejudiced estimate of this Bad Guy, who seemed Bad for other reasons than the mole-cular ones no one suspected.

On one occasion his speaker was of the kind who had no sympathy for homosexuality or show-off or baggy correct clothes in need of the cleaner. He was Admiral Somerville, and they came up together in the lift. Soon after the Admiral spoke of the occasion to one of the higher-ups of the Corporation, his formidable cousin Mary Somerville, Director of Schools Broadcasting; he asked to be delivered from even a lift journey again with such a person. He told his cousin bluffly and indignantly and sarcastically that between the hall and the studio floor he had instinctively placed his backside against the wall of the lift.

That was one man's Guy Burgess. If Admiral Somerville was still alive when Guy Burgess ran off to Moscow, he must have wondered – like everyone else who had dealings with Guy – what on earth shrewd Russians made of this Englishman, why on earth they supposed he could be useful.

That flitting of Burgess and Maclean to Moscow had a sequel for me, and for Stephen Spender's brother Humphrey, the painter. *Picture Post* asked me to write a piece about Wiltshire, which Humphrey was to illustrate with his photos. Humphrey had trouble with his camera. The winding mechanism jammed, and Humphrey had to find somewhere lightless enough to allow him to open up the camera without spoiling the exposures he had made so far. We tried a pub first near Longleat. No good. Humphrey asked if there was a photographer, in Warminster, which was only a few minutes away. There was, we set off, found the photographer, and I sat in the car and waited while Humphrey opened up the camera in the dark room. Suddenly I was aware of a presence, in a shabby macintosh, gesturing through the window. I opened it and the presence displayed a card which showed that he was a plain clothes man from the Warminster Police Station. Like every other policeman in or out of uniform and every journalist he was looking for Burgess and Maclean, and thought he had found them. Was it my car? It wasn't. Was it Mr Spender's car? No, it was a hire car. Where was Mr Spender? In the photographer's dark room.

'Spender?' said the policeman, doubtfully, 'Spender? Haven't I seen something about Burgess and Maclean and Spender?' He had, no doubt, in the *Daily Express*, which had discovered that Stephen Spender knew the fugitives. Stephen had been interviewed by the *Express*.

We let his doubting enquiry float off into the air without comment. How intrigued that policeman would have been if he had realized as well that Burgess and I had been colleagues.

The shabby policeman disappeared through a side door. Humphrey and the shabby policeman re-appeared. 'This fool,' said Humphrey, 'thinks that we are Burgess and Maclean.' We had to search our pockets for proof that we were not Burgess and Maclean.

The *Daily Express*, that day, was offering a reward of £2000 for information about the missing diplomats. The publican at whose inn we had called, thought we were the right age, and associated cameras with spies. He had phoned the police.

We cleared ourselves. 'You'll have to wait,' said the policeman. 'Your descriptions have gone out to every police car in the district. We must tell them to lay off.' We waited for an hour, by request, and then moved off down the Warminster street. At once another police car darted from a side street, and our work of convincing policemen that we were spies for *Picture Post*, but not for Russia, had to be repeated.

The question I propounded as we drove off home at last was which of us was which: did the policeman think I was Burgess? I hoped not. We were both plump, though, and of the same build.

31 – PEVSNER

Nikolaus Pevsner, who was my next door neighbour for some years on the edge of Hampstead Heath, was sitting on a bench in a high passage deep inside the National Gallery, waiting to enter the Director's office. He was bending intently over a small notebook, when a hand lighted on his shoulder, and the voice of the Director, Kenneth Clark, said into his ear *'Immer fleissig, Herr Doktor, immer fleissig.'*

Pevsner's notebook was something of a joke among his friends. The life of that neat methodical man depended, we would all say, on that notebook of memoranda and appointments.

He told us himself about that encounter with Clark, an innocent little tale, it seemed, yet there was a little more to it than might appear – on both sides. He felt it not only as a mild joke against himself and his known habits, but as a residue of a certain dislike – perhaps that is too strong – a certain resentment against this semi-refugee's incursion into English art affairs.

There was no doubt of the still youngish Pevsner's admiration, genuine if tempered, for the arts of this off-shore island. Before he came to England in advance of the main emigration and anti-semitic persecution, the head of the arts department at Göttingen University had encouraged him in the study of art in England, where he might, if necessary, find a haven. He came to England, I suppose on that first occasion, with a letter of introduction to John Meade Faulkner, whom he knew of only as the honorary librarian of Durham Cathedral, so to Durham he travelled. He found Faulkner's eighteenth-century house on the cathedral rock. Faulkner was out, so he left his introductory note with the butler, together, at the butler's request, with the telephone number of his hotel, already rather surprised that a cathedral librarian could afford the wages of a butler.

A call came through soon enough asking him to dinner. The same butler showed him into the drawing-room. He waited and looked around, and had time to be still more astonished at the medieval and other treasures around the room. What a wonderful place England must be, where cathedral librarians lived in such expensively tasteful grandeur, and drank, he soon discovered when he and Faulkner sat to dinner, such exceptional claret. It was only afterwards he discovered that Faulkner was a millionaire (having made his money as an armament manufacturer) as well as a novelist, a poet and a scholar.

Pevsner looked to art studies and design activities for an uneasy living, having a wife and children to support as best he could in this alien country. His valiant wife, small dark, sharp-faced, had something of an iron will, and was the thriftiest woman I have ever met. She used to darn holes in dish cloths. Tactless she was, and caused her husband some embarrassment by remembering aloud her *Deutschtum* in the wrong company, complaining that if she had not married a Jew she would still be in Germany (I fancy she would have darned holes in dish cloths even in Germany).

What caused faint enduring resentment, which never quite died away with some people, was the existence and extraordinary progress and benison of his architectural guides, county by county, parish by parish, and especially parish church by parish church. They were an adaptation of German guides which listed the good things throughout Germany (though without much detail) and they were seen as interfering with the cosy art amateurism of English church-crawling. Mistakes were pounced upon with some glee, occasional intimations, in this or that department of medieval design, of Continental superiority were disliked. Once a rather scornful, not to say bitchy review of one of Pevsner's books appeared in *The Times Literary Supplement*, in the days when all the reviews were anonymous. It didn't take long to pierce the anonymity and Pevsner very soon discovered who the writer was, one of the principal church-crawling sentimentalists of the day, notable for his anti-Pevsnerism, for his dislike that someone – and at that a foreigner – should be substituting professionalism, professional scholarship, for cosy amateurism. The reviewer was John Betjeman.

When the phoney war was on, and bombs were vaguely expected, I spent nights with the Pevsners – till the all-clear sounded in their coal-hole under our common access pavement, garnished with rugs, and when at last two hard-faced Bow Street runners arrived in the early hours of the morning to take him off to his short-lived internment on the Isle of Man, I managed, clutching my pyjama trousers, to catch them up with the best parting present I could quickly think of, which was an elegant little edition, a new edition, of Shakespeare's Sonnets.

I doubt if he ever read them; a suspicion which is part of my own slight case against Nika Pevsner. Like so many art-historians he struck me as not much interested in the active qualities of art – of pictorial art. He was an art-academic decidedly, who might, I used sometimes to suspect, have been as much at home editing a *History of Worthless Art* as in editing a history of art of the profundity of life, and image-making. (When they were taken off to the Isle of Man, Nika and other German academics and art historians lost no time in organizing lecture courses.) Then I cannot deny that in an art sense he inclined to be time-serving. He was expert in the scholarship of Mannerism before he left Germany, but Mannerist studies were hardly going to advance him in a country where they scarcely knew the meaning of the term. The Modern Movement – that was better. The new architecture was something England was waking to. They knew all about stainless steel tubes in Germany, and here was a subject in which the English could be instructed. Wasn't England rubbing its eyes and waking to architecture in general, and so much so that if you wanted honour and advancement architecture and architectural history were the thing? How is it that the study of architecture was noticed and pursued at last? It used to be said that the only two architects the English had ever heard of were Sir Christopher Wren and Clough Williams-Ellis, the romantic who thought up and then realized Portmeirion on the Welsh coast, a comfy architectural arty nest for the well-to-do and æsthetically well informed, or fashionably informed, especially when Venice and Florence were out of reach.

Who, close to No. 10, was sold, not so much on architecture, not so much on modern novelty among the Dutch and the Austrians and the Germans, but on our own architectural history, which had been so neglected? Knighthoods now abounded.

John Summerson (who began his real life work with an investigation of the white buildings – despised rather than praised hitherto – of John Nash) became Sir J. S. Osbert Lancaster, with a finger here, there and everywhere, in smart art and letters (a close friend of Evelyn Waugh) and journalism, or rather comic draughtsmanship (cartoonlets for the *Daily Express*), John Betjeman, in his role as England's prime church-crawler (as well as England's comic poet in all the old familiar metres), and Jim Richards, who edited the *Architectural Review*, that sumptuous periodical so devoted to old and new in architecture and to architecture in the fabric of English life, as to be known affectionately and familiarly always as *The Archie* – all these architectural writers were sirred; so in time the honour, for so many and such diverse services, had to be extended to the refugee who had been swept off to internment and then released to clear away bomb debris for a while as a London navvy.

Next, though, the Modern Movement over, or interest in it dying down, what about the gathering interest in Victorian Art and Victoriana?

Can scholars like everything? Pevsner – knighted Pevsner – came to ascribe to Victorian art more worth than it possessed, by and large, in his new encouragement of the Victorian Society and the values it looks for and supports and promulgates; it is a fair charge that Pevsner played to a final prejudice and helped to betray a lyrical extension of those deeper 'modern' values we had accented in England only piecemeal. Wonderfully as he helped to professionalize the English study of design and English architectural history, he also encouraged that general reaction and reactionary, restored vulgarism in the arts which so marked our later time.

When the real war was over I sold him the cottage which had

sheltered my own family (and one of his children as well for part of the period of danger). He wanted it for solitude in which, *immer fleissig*, he could write up the results, and finds, he made on his extraordinary excursions, with that determined small wife driving their small car, a pair of waifs, lost at night in dismal stretches of unknown countryside, marooned in a lonely church because the car key had fallen down a crack in some tomb chest, or being turned away – occasionally – by the owner of some historical mansion who wanted no foreign intruder inside his ha-ha.

He sojourned now and then among mountains, big obvious mountains, when he could get to them again. But surroundings meant little to him, unless architectural or urban. He saw little. Libraries – and then lecture-rooms – were this scholar's natural, or unnatural home. One evening he was trying to dig a pit in the cottage garden to take the contents of that earth-closet which Henry Moore had sited for its view. A villager watched him from the lane until he could stand the feeble, scholarly jabs at the soil no longer.

'Let oi do it, Doctor Pevsner,' and he jumped through the elder hedge, and drove the spade into the soft ground, Nika looking on regretfully and apologetically. But then he did tell that story as well against himself.

And now, another strange example of the angry topsyturvydom of our age and its strange transferences, the two of them from the medieval heart of Germany, from Naumberg, the Jewish art historian and his very German wife, find themselves side by side under the untidy turf of an English country churchyard. How little he could have guessed, when he took his doctor's degree in Germany, that the single word *Pevsner* would one day come to have a special familiar meaning for architecture and exploration in foreign England, like Liddell and Scott for Greek or Wisden for cricket or Fowler for correct English.

32 – ROY CAMPBELL

Roy Campbell was – no, Roy Campbell became, in middle age – an oaf. Long vanished in the days after the Second War was the handsome verbally energetic young poet from South Africa, with some lyrical and satirical power (though his line, his mode, wasn't in fact so fresh as it seemed), and a clumsy, mumbling vainglorious oaf had taken his place. Lewis, who had been his friend, and had welcomed him as an ally in his own literary strife, found him now too oafish and too stupid to go on knowing. And he didn't care –

> *The man I am to exact what's due to men,*
> *The man I am to exact it only with the pen –*

for various muscular-literary episodes this fumbling mumbling character credited himself with or was credited with by his friends. Roy was a Highlander, at least by descent, and I must say he reminds me just a little of the aboriginal raw Highlander whom St Peter, in the Lowland ballad, challenged God to manufacture out of a cowpat. One of that first Highlander's first acts was to steal St Peter's knife. God asked him how he was going to live, and the Highlander mumbled he was off to the south to steal sheep. I don't say that rough Roy Campbell was a thief, but in his clumsy way he wouldn't have cared for God's warning – or St Peter's warning – that if he behaved like that, they would soon catch him out and string him up.

He served with me – if he could be said to have served at all – on a not very august body called the BBC Literary Advisory Committee, and the tale of how he arrived there is rather more interesting than the tale of what he did there, or didn't do. He had been more or less down and out, and one or two older writers who should have brought themselves up to date and have known better, persuaded George Barnes (I think) to employ him as a producer in Talks Department, then a flourishing and by no means unintellectual club. My impression, or half-recollection, is that Eliot was one person who recommended him for a job in the department and Desmond MacCarthy another, both having a slightly sneaking admiration for muscle and panache. MacCarthy asked for him to be added to the Advisory Committee – just as well that he should be engaged in something, because there can seldom have been a producer more ignorant or incompetent.

Our meeting place as a committee was, after hours, in the comfortable office far upstairs of one of the controllers. A dinner with good bottles of wine would be rolled in and we would get to work, or rather to hearing a most entertaining recital of some one or other of Desmond's adventures as a young man of letters about London, in the purlieus of Bloomsbury. I remember him keeping us laughing and fascinated when he spent most of our time one evening describing how he had been secretary of the first Post-Impressionist Exhibition at the Grafton Galleries in 1910. Angry Academicians and colonel-like persons would come in and shake their umbrellas at pictures by Picasso and Matisse. Finely, frillily dressed society ladies would lean back on frilly parasols and shrill with laughter at Monet or Léger. MacCarthy's happy device was to provide a quarto note book in which, he said, their objections being so sincere and proper, he would be glad if they would write them down and sign them. No, they wouldn't do *that*.

At one of these meetings on a warm summer evening when something more refreshing than wine was in order, Roy took a metal-capped bottle of beer from the trolley and found there was no opener. 'We'll soon manage that.' He pulled out a drawer in the controller's desk, inserted the bottle neck, closed the drawer and in the clumsiest way jerked the bottle down. It slipped and the sharp-edged stopper widely and obviously scored the veneered front of the desk. Consternation from the controller's secretary, who was our secretary as well. Bluster from Roy, and beer in the drawer, and then from Roy mumble, sulks and silence.

I fell foul of Roy in this way, in a happening or half-happening of which inventions and untrue versions have appeared. In the weekly book review, the radio review I was doing for George Barnes, I had included Auden's selection from Tennyson which had been greeted elsewhere – in the *New Statesman?* – in a brusquely sneering or brusquely reproving fashion by our fellow committee member Desmond MacCarthy. He objected in particular to Wystan Auden's remark that Tennyson was the stupidest of our great poets (which he was). So, though I didn't mention Desmond by name in my broadcast I did quote Tennyson's line about 'You chorus of indolent reviewers'. Roy heard it, or heard of it, and next morning when I was hurrying to an appointment in a favourite BBC coffeeshop just down the road from Broadcasting House, who should I see stalking unsteadily up the wide pavement but Roy, thin-lipped, vulture-lipped or saurian-lipped under his colonial headgear, and waving a knobkerrie as he caught sight of me. I greeted him, to be told in a mumbling cry, 'You've insulted my daddie.'

The momentary expectation or possibility of being hit on the head in Regent Street with a knobkerrie wasn't enticing. Also it was not long since that same knobkerrie had actually been employed to hit Stephen Spender, who was on the platform at some meeting (one out of several episodes which had prompted E. M. Forster to write and complain to the Director-General of the BBC about Roy's antics). But I do not think I need have feared. Semi-coherent Roy was so wobbly that a push could have sent him off the pavement into the ditch. I adjured him (not very bravely or certainly, I must say) not to act the fool, and went on to Yarner's coffee-house feeling a little squeamish, but intact.

I recited this small imbroglio to my waiting friends, one of whom was Antony West, H. G. Wells's son, whose comment was a gruff 'You should have kicked him in the balls.'

But what a meal Roy Campbell made of it, ringing up Desmond MacCarthy, sending a telegram 'Grigson defeated', or words to that effect, to Edith Sitwell, whose champion he had also appointed himself (Edith Sitwell, too, had egged him to some such attack, an encouragement which provoked some exchange of solicitor's letters, and an apology, if a forced one, on her part). How Roy boasted to other friends; and what a meal several friends of his also made in print, in books, in articles about this valiant attack on a scourge of literature.

Roy's bluster or his blustering self-congratulation was seldom reliable but sometimes related to the comic. Years after I told the tale of that episode to a novelist acquaintance. She capped it. When she was a girl she was staying with her step-parents at Arles, I think it was, and Roy came as a guest. The house party went off together to the bull-fight, one of those ungory bull-fights those southern French still indulge in or quieten their appetites with. An extra-tame bull trotted or sauntered into the arena, and looked round. Roy, who fancied himself (with reason? I don't know) as a bull-fighter, declared he would show that lazy, indifferent bull a thing or two, and vaulted over the barrier. The bull noticed him, advanced and without much trouble or much rancour, it seems, pushed him over on to the sand, hoofed him a little, and then bent down and – well, what do you think? licked his face.

Roy got up, and got out, adjusted himself and was then heard to complain 'That bull insulted me! That bull insulted me!'

Perhaps he would have acquitted himself better in his younger days, fresh from Durban.

33 – BASIL TAYLOR

How or why or where Basil Taylor killed himself I never knew or enquired. It was shocking enough to learn that it wasn't the first attempt, and that he had tried shooting himself in one of those soulless hotels outside London Airport; shocking to realize all of a sudden that in some agony and nagging of the mind one of the most honest, most lovable persons I have ever known had vanished so prematurely. He was formidable too, in a quiet way, as editors, gallery directors, publishers, art dealers, BBC producers and grandees discovered when they tried to buy him or use him, only to find that he was never for sale, and never for use except on his own terms when he approved the using or the purpose.

I came to know him in this way. In the Forties, after the war had been in progress for some time, and the National Gallery, crowded for lunchtime concerts and emptied of its pictures, which were stored in old underground slate quarries in Wales, those who ran Talks Department in the BBC realized that there was something to be said for talking, or listening to talk, about what wasn't to be seen. Those who ran Talks Department then were professionals, myself no more than an amateur among them, who consulted each other under or with George Barnes and Christopher Salmon, that is to say they were the 'talks producers', of whom Christopher Salmon was probably the most skilful, the most original and intellectually brilliant who ever served English broadcasting.

Very well, there must be such a series of art talks, which one witty but sceptical producer wanted to call *All My Eye*. We started to look for speakers. There were to be two speakers each time, and for the first programme one obvious and willing choice was Kenneth Clark.

The other? I spent a week-end with Herbert Read and his wife at Seer Green. The other guest was Michael Meyer, afterwards known for his new translations of Ibsen, who said the talks producers should ask a friend of his – they had been at school together at Tonbridge – Basil Taylor. Herbert and I knew nothing of him, had never heard of him, but Michael Meyer was persuasive, and gave me this Basil Taylor's phone number – an Oxford number, since Basil, who was unfit for military service, was a student at the Slade, which had been evacuated to Oxford.

Our arrangement was soon made. We were to meet at eleven o'clock two days later in the foyer of the Mitre, which was still Oxford's select hotel, as it had been for centuries.

What did I expect, waiting there on a bright October morning? Perhaps someone a little dumpy and solid, like his friend Meyer, certainly not the slight, fair creature who sidled in, handsome, shy and seemingly – but that was my mistake – unsure of his inner self. Someone who seemed astonishingly young, and who blushed.

The outcome was a talk about Goya, beautifully delivered in a voice which needed next to no production – talks production was an art of this time, and Basil was to develop, on his own account, into one of the most lucid and listenable-to speakers of the day, later on into a grave and never tedious television performer, whose only rivals or equals were Kenneth Clark and my Hampstead friend John Summerson. He shared the programme which opened this *All My Eye* with Clark. Clark seemed upset at having to divide a brief time with someone so young, and, as he listened to the rehearsal, so perfect, so convinced, so interesting and sincere. Moreover Basil's talk was so evidently the better of the two. I think Clark never forgave this boy as year by year his performances became more dignified and convincing. What we discovered about Basil as we came to know him – 'we' being his fellows in Talks Department, in which he quickly became a trainee – was that if he disapproved, he never quarrelled, he withdrew, he simply withdrew.

I saw much of him in his period as a trainee, whom Christopher Salmon thought the most talented recruit of all his days or years in broadcasting and presentation. One occasion in particular I cannot forget, an occasion when his slow slightly self-deprecating smile spread across his long face, that smile which said, 'You are teasing

me, I know, but I enjoy it.' Basil, John Betjeman and I were in a café
in Tavistock, Basil there as trainee to see how Betjeman went about
preparing for one of his own extraordinary talks (he was to talk about
Baring-Gould, novelist, parson, and writer of hymns, and next day
we were to visit Baring-Gould's old curate, who was then incumbent
of Lew Trenchard, which had been Baring-Gould's parish).

'Goodness,' said J.B. with gravity, 'how extraordinary. Dew-
spoons – silver dew-spoons down here in a Devonshire tea-shop. I
wonder if the waitress knows what they are. Do you know about dew-
spoons, Basil?'

Up went Basil's eyebrows a little.

'Dew-spoons – yes.'

On the table were two or three little silver – or more likely
plated – receptacles, with legs, salt in them.

'Dew-spoons . . .'

'Do you know what they were for? Collecting dew on May Day
morning. Girls took them out into the meadows. A common practice
down here in Devonshire,' and that slow smile began to cross Basil's
thin pink countenance, as Betjeman continued with another and
another scrap of learned invention.

'You will find all about how dew-spoons were used in *Brittania's
Pastorals*, by William Browne of Tavistock, Shakespeare's Devonshire friend.'

Basil knew he was being teased, or entertained, and he was
enjoying it.

In a sketchbook I filled much later when I was with Basil high up in
orange mountains in Grand Canary, I have just found a faded
caricature of Basil, with a note teasing him about some of his
timidities, real or supposed – Basil afraid of losing his money, Basil
afraid of vultures, Basil afraid of missing the boat which would take
us home via Sweden, Basil afraid of catching a chill, Basil scared
about bed bugs, Basil getting too sunburnt, Basil afraid of being
stung by Portugese men-of-war. But *au fond* few people were more
resolute.

I wouldn't say he had had the happiest of childhoods. Part Italian by descent, he came of a peculiar family, the only child of a pair who lived in the same house in Kent and hardly spoke to each other month in, month out, for years. His father, I think, was a China merchant who served as deputy director of shipping in the war; and Basil and I were in the Canaries because his father had been given two passages he couldn't use in a Norwegian Fruit Express boat, the company hoping that he would charter one of their ships for the China run.

Tonbridge School Basil did enjoy, fortunate in a history master who gave him a strong living sense of the interaction of past and present. Cricket he enjoyed, an elegant opening bat, he enjoyed the friendship of Michael Meyer, and of the poet Sidney Keyes. Yet he suffered some peculiar strokes of ill-fortune.

A minor one – but perhaps it wasn't so unimportant to him after all – concerned one of his books. His wife rang me up one evening and asked in a puzzled way if I hadn't had a copy of his book about Constable (whose honesty of life and vision and execution we had so often talked about late into the night, before he was married, much as we had talked, as pioneers almost, about the painting of Stubbs).

I said, Yes, and I was going to write a review of it.

'Is that all?' asked his wife, as well she might, because I had never turned to a page before the acknowledgements and introduction, on which a dedication was divided between myself and another of his friends, with an inscription as well in his own hand. I supposed that the copy had come simply from his publishers. A slight that must have seemed. But he suffered in particular one major stroke of ill-fortune of the oddest kind. The Taylors lived then in a house – an old mill-house on the Medway which he had longed to own and had at last been able to buy. He loved gardening and had perfected a fine garden between house and river. Then one morning, one sunny morning in early October, he walked out and the garden wasn't there, or at least half of it wasn't there. Trees, fruit, flowers, it had slipped and slid down to the river, a heap of rubble and muddle at the water's edge. The garden was sand above slippery clay, and the season had been exceptionally wet.

Add that to his by now matured conviction that so many people in his art world, or his broadcasting world, were so far from honest, so far from what they should have been.

I saved some brilliantly blue gentians from that half-ruined garden, that wreck of a happiness.

34 – BEN NICHOLSON

*Of all painters Giorgione and Mu-Chi are for me
the most poetic.*

*Klee's idea of going for a walk with a line is
rather too pedestrian for my taste and I prefer
Rafael's 'perpetual motion' or flight into eternity.*

True or fancy, half true or improved, many stories have been current
about Ben Nicholson. He didn't encourage artist-talk or chatter about
himself, he was indifferent to the social politics of the art world, in
which he took after his formidable mother, the sister of James Pryde
(Pryde and Ben's father, Sir William Nicholson, were the Beggarstaff
Brothers, those original masters of poster design), who said that art
talk made her sick and feel like going out into the kitchen and
scrubbing the table. He spoke much of his mother (whom Max
Beerbohm described as the result of an affair between Milton and the
Mona Lisa), and less of his father. He grew up to distrust his father's
charm, and though he recognized how good a painter his father was, a
fact which isn't as much allowed as it should be, I found it was no good
asking Ben about Sir William. Ask him, and he might volunteer a little
praise, high praise, but not much of it. That distrust of his father's
celebrated charm lasted, Ben told me once, until he visited his father
in the private asylum where he came to be confined, and found him at
tea-time out in the summer gardens every bit as polite and attentive
and charming to fellow patients, elderly ladies around the tea-trolley,
under the sun-umbrella, as he ever had been to patrons or likely
patrons in the days of his sanity and full success.

To be sure his father's name and fame were rather a trial to him. His
father and mother recognized that they had an extraordinary child,
whose co-ordination of hand and eye was exceptional. His father's
friends, Kipling, Barrie, Max Beerbohm, Orpen, Rothenstein,
realized he was an extraordinary child, but such surrounding

company can drive a child in on himself in extra independence. It was for Barrie, by the way, that Ben painted his first published design, a poster for *Peter Pan*, in 1904 – that takes you back – when Ben was eight years old. I asked Ben if Barrie paid him anything for it. 'Not a penny,' said Ben, and the poster – does a copy of it exist? – was all round London.

Ben's mother did not make things easier when she remarked to Ben in a motherly way that he would never be as good a painter as his father. Ben replied that he painted as well as his father already, if not better.

How far Ben had developed when he said that to his mother I am not sure. Perhaps it was when he was already busy on pastiche in the manner of Vermeer. When I first went to his friend Geoffrey Taylor's house in Dublin, Geoffrey pointed to a large canvas in the hall. Who's that by? And after a guess or two at early names I learnt it was in fact a very early Vermeer-like Ben Nicholson. Then for years and years the name Ben Nicholson was only to be found in books about English painting and books of reference as an addendum to *Nicholson, Sir William*. That would have been irksome, if indeed Ben ever noticed it.

I knew Ben first when he was still married to that underrated lyricist Winifred Nicholson, delicate and fresh painter of flowers in a plain jug of simplified landscapes to match, and earlier – for a short while only, when she and Ben lived in Paris – of some of the most delicious abstracts. Her grandfather was that Earl of Carlisle, George Howard, who was friendly with the Pre-Raphaelites and painted rather badly or weakly in a late Pre-Raphaelite manner. Legend maintains that the wing Ben and Winifred lived in for a time in Naworth Castle was liberally decorated with the Earl's water-colours and that Ben and Winifred came back with screws, a bradawl and a screwdriver from the ironmonger's in Carlisle, screwed the framed water-colours back to front, and then painted their own pictures on the back.

What isn't legend is that Ben, lover of children as he was and of cats (he had plenty of both) and of family life, suited matrimony rather to the needs of what he came to speak of at all times as The Work. Winifred suited Ben's lyrical beginnings, his Cumberland landscapes and Cornish harbours, his fireworks and packs of playing cards, when his danger was to become fixed in a simplified charming naivety. When a stronger modernism took possession of him, after Ben and Winifred had come to know Mirò and Brancusi and Mondrian in Paris – colour and structure – he eventually married the more severe Barbara Hepworth. I knew Winifred and Barbara well, I would almost say, but that would be too large a claim, though Ben and Winifred sent me off to exhibitions of their Abstraction – Création group in Paris. I knew Ben Nicholson better still when Ben and Barbara lived in a white aesthetic puritanism in their studio next to Herbert Read's in the Mall in Hampstead, and not so far from the studio of Henry Moore.

Red was all the more red in that white studio, white against red all the more white. I have a vision still of Barbara in a waterfall of a red skirt beginning high and flowing over a vast pregnancy (triplets), she stands there, in recollection, on a platform about floor level, and looks down on me, and lectures me solemnly and very seriously and acceptably, on the nature of art and the duty of artists and their friends. Special objects were treasured and exhibited in that studio, pencils from newsagents down by the bus-stop, shiny Viennese pencils like barber's poles, up which there wound spirals of red or green or blue, fishing floats coloured in much the same brilliance. Cups and saucers were designed by these two with a special analysis of what happens in shape, ornament and colour when cups of tea are lifted to the mouth. The work outside seemed all the more delicious for this white studio world inside.

They had little money. Ben at this time, in his forties, was not a successful artist. But in that studio there was no sense whatever of stringency. When the war came and they thought it prudent to move to St Ives, it was by subterfuge that they acquired a car for the journey to Cornwall. Ben had a picture on offer for a fair sum. The man who was on the verge, shilly-shallied. Ben told him he must have the picture back, because another collector wanted it; which wasn't true. But the risk paid off, and the car wheezed and rattled to the west, where Barbara made a living at first by stitching black-out curtains.

In time Ben and Barbara Hepworth parted, Barbara's severity of purpose having much helped, Ben reflected, in formulating the severity of his own mature aesthetic, his cut-outs, his circles and plateaus, his excavations within the frame, or rather the picture space. Later, when we had driven one day to Tours, Ben regarded the great river again – he had spent some time at Tours as a child recovering from illness and learning French – and said that his plateau and cut-out pictures, his reliefs, had to some degree grown out of his pleasure in the Loire, in the three planes it afforded so often, the water plane superimposed on which was the plane of sandbanks and island, on which again was the plane of willow scrub and still or lazily swaying willow trees.

I came to understand Ben far better in his still alert and vigorous seventies and early eighties, helped him to invent names (how do you name abstract pictures with anything but abstract names? But Ben liked names) in his Swiss studio – Ben was world-famous and wealthy by this time, the days long over when he would come round to Keats Grove in his small car with a Kit Wood and a Ben Nicholson on offer for five pounds the pair; and learnt from him about the Chinese masters he admired, and about the virtues of Dover sole and decaffeinated coffee, and a sleep after lunch.

The Work was in evidence – the concept and the fact. He spoke of The Work as if it were a presence, a second party, or first party, to whom all deference, all attention, was due. All of The Work was catalogued in long card-indexes. Not a picture was forgotten. He was conscious of age, conscious he couldn't last for ever, but while he lasted there were pictures to be painted, new subjects to be discovered which could be painted seriatim, in one version and another. There were letters to be written about The Work, poems to be enjoyed – poems in particular by Stevie Smith, high among them 'Tenuous and Precarious',

Tenuous and Precarious
Were my guardians,
Precarious and Tenuous,
Two Romans . . .

There were children and cats to be amused, puns to be made.

My wife asks her small daughter if she wants some more mushroom soup. 'It depends how much room she has.'

We go to Avebury: our daughter explains that the narrow stones are said to be male, the wide stones, like huge Venuses of Willendorf, are said to be female. 'I see, menhir, woman there.'

A favourite pun, which had made his own children groan 'Ben, not that again!' when he repeated it, explained the origin of the word *beetroot*: the girl's red-faced lover fell into the flooded river, and sank till only his red nose was visible. His last agonized cry was *Be true to me! Be true to me!*

A jug or a goblet was still something to give to him. But you couldn't count on taking him to the right place, or showing him the right thing. I took him to the small Romanesque chapel of Ronsard's priory at Montoire, thinking, hoping, poor fool that I was, that Ben might enjoy some of the tones and forms of the wall-paintings. He didn't notice them. But he did notice and enjoy and draw a circular window which narrowed in a funnel shape.

His charm was equal to his father's, by all accounts, with manners to match – and a nerve. The entry, once you were past the electric gate, to his studio above Lago Maggiore in the Ticino was by a foyer where he could beat a ping-pong ball around for himself and his cat. Here he received, one day, Princess Margaret, and the Earl of Snowdon, laden with cameras. Ben's greeting was faultless, but before they mounted the stairs, he turned to Snowdon and remarked 'You did see the notice?' Hanging on a row of pegs was a notice which said 'Cameras here, please.' Snowdon divested himself of his cameras and hooked them up.

Speed was something enjoyed by this master of trajectory. One of the last cars he owned, the speed of which, with Ben half white-haired, half bald, at the wheel, scared his passengers, was – pun again – a sports Mercedes-Benz, a make, he said, which ought to be called Ben's Mercedes. He drove it down to the garage in our village in France for some adjustment. Radet *garagiste* walked around it in admiration, touching it a time or two with a chammy leather.

'A wonderful car, m'sieur. Would you mind telling me how much it cost?'

'I haven't an idea,' said Ben, in his good French. 'It was a present from a friend.' That was the kind of question not to ask Ben, whether you kept a garage or a gallery: an intrusion, a liberty. 'Address your questions to me,' he might have said, 'about The Work.'

Ben knew who he was, he knew what his discipline had made of his skill. If he knew that you knew, good . . . If you did not appear to know, well, that was your fault, not his. If someone, some foundation or other gave him a prize, how sensible of them – on behalf of The Work. Yet another honour had accrued to Henry Moore? Well, Henry was an old friend, but Henry would accept anything, this or that; the offer of which, though plenty came Ben's way, would really have been rather insulting to The Work. And how tiresome museum officials could be, who came out to see him, and then preferred engaging him in art-talk, art-chatter, instead of coming with him to be shown some favourite ruin, some favourite sprawl of white columns, some favourite place for a picnic. He was the least scratchy or vindictive of men, but how, in the interest of The Work and its triumph, remembering when he had had to adjust himself to not always sympathetic dealers, he enjoyed telling his London dealer on the long distance phone that every exhibit in his coming show must be illustrated in the catalogue.

'*Everything?*'

'*Yes, everything.*'

'*In colour?*'

'*Of course, in colour. Everything.*'

'*But –* '

His insistence was entirely firm, and altogether polite, though he might explain that was the condition on which they had the show. There were galleries waiting for it, galleries who would jump at it in Zürich, in Basel, Amsterdam, Hanover, in Tokyo, in New York . . .

It might sound as if this small, dapper, vigorous artist, slightly old-fashioned in his rakishly worn beret and soft-soled canvas shoes and bright coloured shirt and trousers, was some form of outrageous monster, an unexampled egoist (he was in fact the most generous of artists, the most generous of friends), but what company he was, how glad one always was to see him.

Thinking of Ben, now he had 'popped off' – that was one word of half jocular, slightly old-fashioned slang he would indulge in, about his inevitable end – there came back to me again and again the details of one blessedly sunny and happy day. Where would he like to go?

Well, why not Bath? It was years since he had seen Bath. He would have a look around Bath by himself. Where would we meet? On the grass verge below the Royal Crescent. How rare and wonderful the Crescent is, for England what a rare masterpiece of monumentality, Ben insists, when we find him sitting by one of the willows, an hour, or two hours later. We move off to eat lunch in The Hole in the Wall, Ben first going into one of the Bath antique shops on the other side of the street and emerging with a brown paper parcel which he carried with much care.

Home again in our Wiltshire farmhouse, this old, old man felt chilly, and decided to sit for a while in the kitchen, into which he carried that parcel, unwrapped it, revealing an exceptionally fine and large glass goblet. He poised the goblet near the window, the light shining into its curves, which made the most delicate of criss-crossing lines. There in solitude he sat and drew that goblet until supper time.

For some of the unquavering harmonies of line and form derived – in part – from that goblet and from that day of ordinary happiness and content, and from a lifetime of disciplined obedience to The Work, see reproductions of the late Sixties and early Seventies in Nicholson catalogues of the Galerie Beyeler at Basel, and in John Russell's huge book of Ben's drawings, paintings and reliefs.

Mention of that goblet in the Bath antique shop and the Wiltshire kitchen reminds me again of Ben's pleasure (matched by Auden's) in simple and delicate eating, in dishes with the taste, so to say, of fine drawings. He liked the actions of cooking, too. He would sit in the kitchen and watch my wife cutting and mixing and kneading, and bending to the grill or the oven, explaining that kitchen activities were a part of life, part of the changing shapes and grace of being, as interesting to Ben as the shape and grace and movement – and colours – involved in the playing of billiards and snooker, or fives or tennis.

He was good at those games; and good at actual cooking as well, I suspect. Anyhow a week or two after that last but one visit to us in Wiltshire, Ben sent my wife a favourite recipe – an excellent recipe too – for brown bread ices. No surprise really, and no contradiction.

Ben's tastes – in everything – were his own. The essence of him was independence, and I reflect that he was one who had always been his own master, staying only a short while at school (where cricket was about all he enjoyed) and at the Slade.

Like every great artist, pleased with its triumphs, disappointed with – in himself – any shortcoming in his visual experience of it, Ben was in love with existence. There was an occasion – goblets again or jugs and bowls – when Ben took friends from Cambridge to an Alpine point higher than his Maggiore studio, a point, Ben said, from which they could see the world. While they had their fill of the world, their fill of snow and sky and peaks, Ben announced he would begin a new painting of the world when they were back in the studio, and he did: the painting or drawing he settled to, was one of a jug and a bowl.

That wise and gentle art critic Charles Marriott, the only newspaper art critic of Ben's middle career – working for *The Times*, of all papers – who understood and was consistently sympathetic about the modern movement in Europe, once said to me in his old age 'You have only to talk with Ben Nicholson and Henry Moore for a few minutes to realize they are superior persons.'

I blessed Charles Marriott for that choice – that exactly right choice – of adjective. They are rare, these superior persons, and what luck I have had, when I look back, to have known in my day, those two superior persons; and five more as well, I would reckon.